Churches
of
Today

In the Light of Scripture

by
L. G. Tomlinson

ISBN 1-58427-173-6

Guardian of Truth Foundation
P.O. Box 9670
Bowling Green, Kentucky 42102
1-800-428-0121
www.truthbooks.net

DEDICATION

TO THAT ONE
WHO THROUGH THE LEAN YEARS HAD
FAITH IN ME WHEN OTHERS DOUBTED;
WHO WITH UNHERALDED DEVOTION
STOOD LOYALLY BY WHEN THE GOING
WAS HARD; WHO OFFERED WORDS OF
ENCOURAGEMENT WHEN THE WAY WAS
DIM; WHO, AS THE WONDERFUL HELP-
MATE GOD HAS GIVEN ME, POURED OUT
OF THE CRUSE OF HER LIFE THE OIL OF
HEALING LOVE, THIS BOOK IS AFFEC-
TIONATELY DEDICATED.

CONTENTS

THE GREAT SALVATION

Section II.

DENOMINATIONAL TEACHING AND PRACTICES IN THE LIGHT OF SCRIPTURE

Section III.

THE RESTORATION MOVEMENT IN THE LIGHT OF SCRIPTURE

Section IV.

BIBLICAL TEACHINGS

FOREWORD

There is always a reason for the writing of every book. Indeed, if there is no good, impelling reason for writing a book it had better be left unpenned since the world is already full of good books and we find time to read so few of them.

The impelling reasons for writing this book, briefly stated, are:

I.

To help those who are confused and lost in the way to find the light. So much confusion exists today because of division that the honest seeker after truth finds himself in the maze of uncertainty. This church says, "This is the way to believe and practice;" that church says, "Our way is the right one to follow in matters of faith and discipline;" still another says, "Neither of these ways is apostolic, come with us." To further add to his difficulty, the earnest seeker hears others say, "Oh, it doesn't make any difference; one is just as good as another; all roads lead to the same place." This book is an honest effort to assist such persons to diligently compare the different churches with the Bible and thereby find which one follows the straight and narrow way that leads home, even though there be only a few that find it.

II.

To offer to those who are seeking after truth a handbook containing the cardinal teachings of the various denominations and to show what the Bible has to say concerning these principles. These doctrines, held sacred by the various denominations, have been enumerated with a studied effort to be fair, impartial and truthful in their presentation. Personality has been pushed aside and the light of the Scriptures has been sought. The least possible comment has been made, barely enough being given to focus more clearly the light of Scriptural truth upon the teaching in hand.

Perhaps now and then a principle is stated which some member of a denomination may not believe, or which his particular church has ceased to uphold; but the principle has been stated here because, while one branch of a denomination may deny teaching it, another branch does uphold it. The truth of this becomes immediately apparent when it is remembered that there are two different kinds of Catholic Churches, at least four different kinds of Episcopal Churches, several kinds of Lutheran Churches, nine or ten kinds of Baptist Churches, some eighteen kinds of Methodist Churches, over a dozen kinds of Presbyterian Churches, several kinds of Seven Day Adventist Churches, to say nothing of the numerous divisions of the smaller bodies.

Again, since human creeds and books of discipline are fallible, they are undergoing a constant change and for that reason a careful effort has been made to state the broad principles generally accepted.

The very fact that these creeds have been changed so often only serves to show they are human and this fact ought to encourage the honest seeker after truth to flee to the Bible and that alone.

Then, too, it may be found by such a seeker that his denomination does teach these principles, but he has grown beyond his denomination in his search for truth.

Wherever it has been deemed necessary to sustain principles stated reference has been made to the creed, book of discipline or writings of the denomination considered, a list of which has been given in the Bibliography of this book. Occasionally, however, a principle held sacred by some particular denominational body has been stated without giving a citation from their creed or book of discipline, but the reason for so doing is that the principle is so well sustained by the practice of that body that it is familiar to all and needs no further substantiation.

8

III.

To restore the authority of the Scriptures. There was a day when one heard it often said, "Oh, it is all a matter of interpretation." That day is gone, if it ever had a right to exist. Peter said, "No prophecy of Scripture is of private interpretation" (II Peter 1: 20). The curse of Christendom has been interpretation. We are not to interpret the Scriptures, but to accept them as they have been left to us by God Himself. Christ said, "All authority has been given unto me in heaven and on earth" (Matt. 28: 18), and that authority is expressed in Christ's words, for He said, "The word that I have spoken, the same shall judge him in the last day" (John 12: 48). If a man, then, is to be judged by Christ's word in the last day, it behooves him to make it his rule of faith and practice in this life.

IV.

To restore the unity of the one church of apostolic pattern. Only by the restoration of the authority of the Scriptures will God's people be united. Amos said, "Can two walk together except they be agreed?" (Amos 3: 3). And no two can be agreed by taking different authorities.

The origin of sin came from a rebellion against the authority of God and the sin of division today has come about by accepting human authority as manifested in human creeds in the place of the supreme authority of the Scriptures. The law and the testimony form the only basis for unity. As human creeds, confessions of faith and books of discipline have brought about apostasy and division, nothing less than a rejection of human creeds and decrees of church councils and the accepting of a "thus saith the Lord" for every tenet of belief and reason for practice will ever restore the one church Christ established. As the church is not a democracy where the members may legislate their own laws, but an autocracy where Christ and His Word are supreme authority, this book is written to help the earnest follower of Christ "to speak where the Bible speaks and be silent where it is silent." ✓

9

V.

To thoroughly furnish the workman in Christ's vineyard unto all good works. Paul's admonition to Timothy needs to be earnestly heeded today. "From a child thou hast known the holy Scriptures, which are able to make thee wise unto salvation through faith which is in Christ Jesus. All Scripture is given by inspiration of God and is profitable for doctrine, for reproof, for correction, for instruction in righteousness: that the man of God may be perfect, thoroughly furnished unto all good works" (II Tim. 3: 15-17). Again, "Study to show thyself approved unto God, a workman that needeth not to be ashamed, rightly dividing the Word of truth." This book is written that every follower of Christ may be able to "sanctify the Lord God in his heart and be ready always to give an answer to every man that asketh him a reason for the hope that is in him with meekness and fear."

VI.

Finally, if this book shall be of any assistance in winning one soul to Christ or of teaching one person the way of the Lord more perfectly, that in itself will be reason enough for offering it to the world.

THE AUTHOR.

SECTION I.

The Great Salvation

NONE SAVED BY THE OLD TESTAMENT LAW

1. Both the Jew and Gentile were under sin after Jesus had shed His blood, showing that nothing but obedience to the Gospel could save(Rom. 3: 9).
2. No one was justified by the deeds of the law (Rom. 3: 20).
3. "For if they which are of the law be heirs, faith is made void, and the promise made of none effect" (Rom. 4: 14).
4. We are dead to the law by the body of Christ in order that we may be married to Christ (Rom. 7: 4).
5. The Old Testament law was the "law of sin and death", while the "law of life" is in Christ (Rom. 8: 2).
6. The law left all in unbelief because it was not of faith (Rom. 11: 32).
7. The Old Testament law killed, but the New Testament law gives life through Christ (II Cor. 3: 6).
8. The Old Testament law "written and graven in stones" was the "ministration of death" (II Cor. 3: 7, 8).
9. The Old Testament law was the "ministration of condemnation" (II Cor. 3: 9).
10. The Old Testament Scriptures were "veiled" to all those under the old law (II Cor. 3: 14).

11. The works of the law justified no one (Gal. 2: 16).
12. If righteousness came by the law, then Christ died in vain (Gal. 2: 21).
13. There was no Holy Spirit under the law to guide unto all truth (Gal. 3: 1-5).
14. All under the Old Testament law were under a curse (Gal. 3: 10).
15. No one is justified by the law in the sight of God (Gal. 3: 11, 12).
16. Christ has "redeemed" us from the curse of the law (Gal. 3: 13).
17. The law made no one an heir, neither did it offer an eternal inheritance (Gal. 3: 18).
18. If there had been a law which could have given life, righteousness should have been by the law and not by the Gospel (Gal. 3: 21).
19. After the law had come and gone, all, Jew and Gentile, were still under sin (Gal. 3: 22).
20. While the law was still in force, faith had not yet come (Gal. 3: 23).
21. The law was a schoolmaster to bring us to Christ (Gal. 3: 24, 25, 26).
22. It is those who have been baptized into Christ that are in Christ. Those under the law were without a Saviour (Gal. 3: 27-29).
23. The Jews had to be redeemed from the curse of the law to receive the adoption of sons (Gal. 4: 1-5).
24. Those who return to the law, return to the weak and beggarly elements and desire to return to bondage (Gal. 4: 9).
25. Paul was afraid he had bestowed labor in vain upon the Jews that wanted to return to the law (Gal. 4: 11).
26. Paul, using the allegory of the bondwoman and the freewoman, told us to cast out the law because the sons of the law could not be heirs with the sons of the Gospel (Gal. 4: 21-31).

27. Only Christ makes us free. The law is a "yoke of bondage" (Gal. 5: 1).

28. Those claiming to be justified by the law are fallen from grace (Gal. 5: 4).

29. The hope of righteousness was never by the law (Gal. 5: 5, 6).

30. Paul wished those were impotent who taught salvation by the old law (Gal. 5: 12).

31. Christ's death did not save the Jew, but only broke down the middle wall of partition (the law) between Jew and Gentile (Eph. 2: 13-15).

32. The law is called the "enmity" and Christ slew it, taking it out of the way (Eph. 2: 16).

33. The law opened no completed way to God (Eph. 2: 14-18).

34. We must depend upon grace to secure salvation (Titus 2: 11).

35. The law made nothing perfect (Heb. 7: 19).

36. The law was but a shadow of good things to come (Heb. 10: 1).

37. The law is not of faith (Gal. 3: 12); therefore the law could save no one (Heb. 11: 6).

38. John the Baptist, the greatest man the law could produce, was less than the least under the Gospel (Matt. 11: 11).

THE ONE WAY

1. Job prophesied of one way (Job 28: 7).

2. David spoke of one path (Psa. 16: 11).

3. Solomon spoke of one path (Prov. 4: 18).

4. Isaiah prophesied of one path (Isa. 35: 8).

5. Jeremiah foretold one way (Jer. 32: 39).

6. Christ said there is one way leading unto everlasting life (Matt. 7: 13, 14).

7. Christ said, "I am the Way" (John 14: 6).

8. Christ said there is one door (John 10: 9).

9. Christ said there is one Shepherd (John 10: 16).
10. Christ said there is one fold (John 10: 16).
11. Christ built one church (Matt. 16: 18).
12. Christ commissioned the preaching of one Gospel (Mark 16: 15, 16).
13. Paul knew but one Gospel (Gal. 1: 8, 9).
14. There is one body (Eph. 4: 4).
15. There is one Spirit (Eph. 4: 4; I Cor. 12: 4).
16. There is one hope (Eph. 4: 4).
17. There is one Lord (Eph. 4: 5).
18. There is one faith (Eph. 4: 5).
19. There is one baptism (Eph. 4: 5).
20. There is one God (Eph. 4: 6).
21. There is one doctrine (Matt. 7: 28; John 7: 16, 17; Acts 2: 42; 5: 28; Rom. 6: 17; Eph. 4: 14; I Tim. 1: 3; II Tim. 4: 2, 3).
22. There are many doctrines of men (Matt. 15: 9; Col. 2: 20-22; Heb. 13: 9).
23. There are many doctrines of devils (I Tim. 4: 1).
24. A preacher must continue in the doctrine of Christ to save himself and those who hear him (I Tim. 4: 16).
25. We are not to receive into our homes or bid God-speed to those who bring doctrine other than that of Christ (II John 10, 11).

Summary

1. ONE way, not many ways.
2. ONE path, not many paths.
3. ONE door, not many doors.
4. ONE fold, not many folds.
5. ONE church, not many churches.
6. ONE Gospel, not many gospels.
7. ONE doctrine, not many doctrines.
8. ONE body, not many bodies.
9. ONE Spirit, not many spirits.

14

10. ONE hope, not many hopes.
11. ONE Lord, not many Lords.
12. ONE faith, not many faiths.
13. ONE baptism, not many baptisms.
14. ONE God and Father, not many Gods and many Fathers.

Division among Christ's followers are unScriptural and contrary to Christ's prayer (John 17: 20, 21; I Cor. 1: 10-13).

THINGS TO WHICH SALVATION IS ASCRIBED

We who believe are saved:
1. By Christ's words (John 6: 63).
2. By the Holy Spirit (John 16: 8; Titus 3: 5).
3. By faith (Rom. 10: 10).
4. By repentance (Luke 13: 3; II Peter 3: 9).
5. By baptism (Mark 16: 16; I Peter 3: 21; Titus 3: 5).
6. By God (John 3: 16; Titus 2: 11).
7. By Christ's works (John 20: 30, 31).
8. By calling on His name (Acts 2: 21).
9. By Christ's name (Acts 4: 12).
10. By Christ's resurrection (Rom. 4: 25).
11. By Christ's death (Rom. 5: 6).
12. By Hope (Rom. 8: 24).
13. By confession of faith (Rom. 10: 10).
14. By hearing (Rom. 10: 15-17).
15. By preaching (I Cor. 1: 18).
16. By fire (I Cor. 3: 15).
17. By the Gospel (I Cor. 15: 1, 2).
18. By love (Gal. 5: 6).
19. By grace (Eph. 2: 8).
20. By ourselves (Phil. 2: 12).
21. By the love of the truth (II Thes. 2: 10).

22. By Christ (I Tim. 1: 15).
23. By heeding and continuing in the doctrine (I Tim. 4: 16).
24. By God's mercy (Titus 3: 5).
25. By obedience (Heb. 5: 9).
26. By Christ's blood (Heb. 9: 14).
27 By works of faith (James 2: 24).

NOTE: The question is not, which one of these will save; but all combined insure to us salvation.

NOTE: How shall we escape if we neglect so great salvation? (Heb. 2: 3).

SECTION II.

Denominational Teachings and Practices in the Light of Scripture

***

ROMAN CATHOLIC

The Catholic Church had an embryonic beginning. The early church departed from the simplicity of a congregational form of government, guided by the New Testament as the only Rule of Faith and Practice, and permitted more and more authority to be vested in the bishops of the various churches. By the middle of the second century the church was well united under the authority of the bishops who gradually came to be regarded as successors to the apostles. In opposition to the heresies creeping in, the church came to be called the "catholic" or "universal" church. The adoption of a creed as the rule of faith and practice in the third century put forth the bud, the union of church and state under Constantine; and the writing of the Nicene Creed in 325 brought forth the flower; while the setting up a "papa" or pope as the ecclesiastical head of the church, culminating in the doctrine of his infallibility in 1870, produced the fruit as manifested in the Catholic Church of today.

The Catholic Church suffered a severe split in 1054 when it divided into the Greek and Roman Catholic Churches. This was brought about partly through the jealousy between the bishop of Constantinople and the bishop of Rome, but principally over the "Filioque" addition to the Nicene creed made by the Roman Church.

The full official title of the Greek Church is, "The

Holy Orthodox Catholic Apostolic Eastern (or Oriental)
Church". The full official name of the Roman Church is,
"The Holy Catholic Apostolic and Roman Church".

ROMAN CATHOLIC TEACHING

I. CONCERNING THE BIBLE CATHOLICISM TEACHES:
1. That tradition, apocryphal writings, etc., are
to be accepted on a par with the Bible.

THE BIBLE TEACHES:
1. That the Scriptures are alone sufficient (Deut.
4: 2; Isa. 8: 20).
2. That the commandments of God are made of no
effect by the traditions of men (Matt. 15: 3, 6).
3. That those who teach the commandments of men
as doctrine worship God in vain (Matt. 15: 9).
4. That there is no redemption in corruptible things
received by tradition from the fathers (I Peter
1: 18).
5. That the Scripture is sufficient to make the man
of God perfect (II Tim. 3: 15-17).
6. That there is to be no addition to, or subtraction
from the Word of God (Rev. 22: 18, 19).

II. That the Catholic Church only has the right to
interpret the Scriptures.

THE BIBLE TEACHES:
1. The Scriptures are for all (John 5: 39; Acts
17: 11; I Peter 2: 2; II Peter 1: 19; Rev. 1: 3).
2. The Scriptures are not to be specially inter-
preted (II Peter 1: 20; R. V. margin).

III. That they alone have the right Bible.
NOTE: Why do they lock it up, then, in the Vat-
ican? Why do not the people use it instead of a
prayer book?

CONCERNING THE CHURCH

I. CATHOLICISM TEACHES:
1. That the Catholic Church is the only true apostolic church.

18

THE BIBLE:

1. The true church (in the figure of the star-crowned woman) went into hiding 1260 days (Rev. 12: 1-7).

   NOTE: A day in prophetic history represents a year (Ezek. 4: 5, 6).

2. Catholic Church came into being while the true church was in hiding.

3. The Catholic Church is a union of church and state. There was no union of church and state until Constantine in 325 A. D.; so the Catholic Church could not have existed before that date.

4. The church for the first three centuries was called the Church of Christ (Rom. 16: 16), Church of God (I Cor. 1: 1), Church of the First Born (Heb. 12: 23), etc. It was never called the Catholic Church until the time of the apostacy.

5. The Catholic Church is defined as the apostate church in the Scriptures and is called the Mother of Harlots (Rev. 17: 1-18).

   (1.) She is a city on seven hills (Rev. 17: 9, 18).

   (2.) NOTE: Rome, the center of Catholicism, is built on seven hills.

   (3.) She sits on many waters—peoples, multitudes, nations and tongues (Rev. 17: 1, 15).

   (4.) She has the world drunk with the wine of her spiritual fornication (Rev. 17: 1, 2).

   (5.) She is drunk with the blood of martyrs Rev. 17: 6).

   NOTE: Read the history of her inquisitions.

   (6.) She is Mysterious (Rev. 17: 5).

   NOTE: Has there ever been anything more mysterious than the Catholic Church?

(7.) She is called Babylon (Rev. 17: 5).

> NOTE: Babylon means confusion. She is the cause of all spiritual confusion in the world. She changed the name, form of government, act of baptism and is the originator of all human creeds. All these changes have thrown the world into spiritual confusion.

(8.) She is called the "Mother of Harlots."

> NOTE: In her catechism she teaches she is the mother of all churches.

(9.) Therefore the Catholic Church is not the only true apostolic church, but she is the APOSTATE church.

II. That Peter founded the church at Rome and that the church is built on him.

THE BIBLE:

1. Only the apostles had power to confer spiritual gifts (Acts 6: 1-6; Acts 8: 12-18; 19: 6, 7; II Tim. 1: 6).

2. Paul longed to visit the church at Rome in order that he might impart unto them some spiritual gift (Rom. 1: 10, 11).

NOTE: This shows that the church at Rome was not organized by any apostle or it would have already possessed spiritual gifts.

3. Therefore Peter did not found the church at Rome, for had he done so, having the power of an apostle, he would have conferred spiritual gifts upon the church.

4. Peter denies that the church was built on him (I Peter 2: 4-6).

5. The church is built on "Petra"—meaning rock. Christ is the "Petra" or "rock" (I Cor. 10: 4).

THE PAPACY

I. That Peter was the first Pope and head of the church.

The Bible:

1. Peter denied being head of the church. He said Christ is the head (I Peter 2: 4-6).
2. Paul said Christ is the head of the church (Eph. 5: 23; Col. 1: 18).
3. Peter did not claim superiority (I Peter 5: 1).
4. Even Paul, speaking of himself, said he was not behind the chiefest apostles (II Cor. 11: 5).
5. James, and not Peter, presided at the first church council (Acts 15: 13, 19).
6. Christ taught the apostles not to exercise dominion over any one (Matt. 20: 25, 26).
7. First "Papa" or pope mentioned was in the sixth century.

II. That the popes are successors to Peter.

The Bible:

1. Only one case of apostolic succession in the Scriptures (Acts 1: 15-26).
2. The successor of an apostle must have companied with Christ from the baptism of John to the ascension of Christ (Acts 1: 21, 22).
3. None today, or immediately following the days of the apostles, could meet the requirements of an apostle or the successor of an apostle. Therefore it is Scripturally plain that there is to be no apostolic succession.
4. When James was beheaded they did not meet and select one to take his place, as in the case of Judas (Acts 2: 15-26; 15: 1-29).

III. That the pope is the Vicar or representative of Christ on earth.

THE BIBLE:

1. The only personal representative of Christ on earth is the Comforter or Holy Spirit (John 14: 15-17; 26: 16: 7).

2. NOTE: While all Christians are in a sense representatives they are not representatives as is the Holy Spirit.

IV. That the pope is infallible.

1. Paul rebuked Peter because he was at fault, therefore Peter was fallible (Gal. 2: 11-14).

NOTE: Some Catholics claim that Peter was only infallible in relation to spiritual things; therefore the popes are only infallible in spiritual commands, but not necessarily in morality. It can not be too well noted that Peter was at fault in a spiritual matter.

V. That the popes and priest should live in an unmarried state.

THE BIBLE:

1. Peter was married and therefore could not have been a Catholic pope (Matt. 8: 14).

2. Paul said Peter had a wife (I Cor. 9: 5).

VI. That the pope should be called "Holy Lord God, the pope."

THE BIBLE:

1. Peter would not have made a good pope, for he would not allow men to worship him (Acts 10: 25, 26).

2. Paul, Peter's equal, would not allow men to worship him (Acts 14: 14, 15).

3. Christ forbade the worshiping of men (Matt. 4: 10).

4. Not even an angel is to be worshiped by men (Rev. 19: 10; 22: 8, 9).

THE PRIESTHOOD

CATHOLICISM TEACHES:

I. That the priest is the means of access between the sinner and God.

THE BIBLE:

1. There is only one mediator—Christ (I Tim. 2: 5).
2. Christ said, "Come unto me" (Matt. 11: 28).
3. Paul said the only means of access is through Christ's blood (Heb. 9: 14-22; 10: 10-14).
4. Christ has the only unchangeable priesthood (Heb. 7: 11, 12, 22-24).
5. There is only one earthly priesthood (I Peter 2: 5, 9; Rev. 1: 5, 6).

II. That priests should be called "father".

THE BIBLE:

1. Christ said: "Call no man your father (Matt. 23: 9, 10).

III. That priests can absolve from sins, even though sinners themselves (Council of Trent).

THE BIBLE:

1. Forgiveness of sins belongs to the Godhead (Mark 2: 6-10; I John 1: 9; 2: 1).

PURGATORY

CATHOLICISM TEACHES:

I. That there is a place called Purgatory where the dead go to suffer punishment in order to be purified. (Introduced in the sixth century and made a church doctrine in the Council of Florence 1439)

THE BIBLE:

1. The Scriptures teach against this (Heb. 9: 27).
2. Christ shows there is no second chance for the wilful sinner here (Luke 16: 19-31).

3. Bible knows nothing of indulgences either plenary or partial (Heb. 2: 3).

4. No such thing as purgatory ever mentioned in the Scriptures.

NAME

CATHOLICISM TEACHES:

I. That the name to be worn is Catholic.

THE BIBLE:

1. Adam and his wife wore the same name (Gen. 5: 2).

2. Adam is a figure of Christ (Rom. 5: 14; I Cor. 15: 45).

3. Adam's wife, then, is a figure of Christ's wife, the church.

4. Adam and his wife wearing the same name pictured Christ and His wife wearing the same name.

5. Prophesied that a NEW name was to be given by the mouth of the Lord, when salvation went out from Jerusalem and the Gentiles saw His righteousness (Isa. 62: 1, 2).

6. The Prophecy fulfilled.

(1.) Salvation went out from Jerusalem (Acts 2: 1-47).

(2.) The Gentiles saw His righteousness (Acts 10: 1-48; 11: 1).

(3.) The new name given (Acts 11: 25, 26).

(4.) The name "Christ-ian" means belonging to Christ.

7. We are married to Christ (Rom. 7: 4).

8. King Agrippa knew Christ's followers wore the name Christian (Acts 26: 28).

9. Peter said we are to suffer in the name Christian (I Peter 4: 16).

10. No salvation promised in any other name (Acts 4: 12).

SACRAMENTS

<small>CATHOLICISM TEACHES:</small>

I. That there are seven sacraments, five for the living and two for the dead.

   1. The word sacrament comes from Sacramentum", meaning an oath.

<small>THE BIBLE:</small>

1. They are not spoken of as sacraments in the Bible.

2. There are only two ordinances of Christ, Baptism and the Lord's Supper.

BAPTISM

The seven sacraments as taught by the Catholic Church considered.

1. ·The Catholic Church teaches that affusion, or sprinkling is sufficient for baptism.

<small>THE BIBLE:</small>

   (1.) Baptism is a birth (John 3: 5).
   (2.) Baptism is a washing (Acts 22: 16).
   (3.) Baptism is a burial (Rom. 6: 4).
   (4.) Baptism is a planting (Rom. 6: 5).
   (5.) Baptism is a resurrection (Col. 2: 12).
   (6.) There is ONE baptism (Eph. 4: 5).
      NOTE: Paul, who called baptism a burial, planting, washing and a resurrection, said there is ONE baptism. He ought to know.

2. That an infant should be baptized.

<small>THE BIBLE:</small>

   (1.) Believers who repent are to be baptized (Rom. 10: 1; Acts 2: 38; Mark 16: 15, 16).

3. That the infant when baptized should be christ-

ened with the name of a saint and should have a
godfather and a godmother.

THE BIBLE:

    (1.) Where is this doctrine or practice to be
    found anywhere?

PENANCE

CATHOLICISM TEACHES:

I. That the priests can forgive sins committed after
    baptism. (Lateran Council 1215.)

THE BIBLE:

1. Forgiveness of sins belong to the God-head.
(Mark 2: 6-10; I John 1: 9; 2: 1).

II. That sin can be forgiven by paying the priest to
    pray for the forgiveness of sins. Also that sin-
    ners can be prayed out of purgatory by paying
    the priest.

THE BIBLE:

1. Redemption can not be purchased with gifts
of silver or gold (I Peter 1: 18).

CONFIRMATION

CATHOLICISM TEACHES:

I. That in confirmation we receive the Holy Spirit by
    the hands of the bishop.

THE BIBLE:

1. Confirmation as such is not taught.
2. Christ the only one who can pray for the Holy
Spirit to be sent (John 14: 15-17).
3. The Father only can confer the Holy Spirit
(John 14: 15-17).

HOLY EUCHARIST

CATHOLICISM TEACHES:

I. That the bread and fruit of the vine become the
    real body and blood of Christ at the consecra-

tion of the mass (Adopted by the church in the Council of Lateran 1215).

THE BIBLE:

1. Christ was materially present "outside" of the bread and the fruit of the vine when He said, "This is my body," and "This is my blood" (Matt. 26: 26-28).

2. When Christ said He was a vine (John 15: 1) and a door (John 10: 9), He did not become a literal vine or door.

II. That the Lord's Supper is a sacrifice.

THE BIBLE:

1. The Lord's Supper commemorates a "FIN-ISHED" sacrifice (Luke 22: 19).

2. Repeating of Christ's sacrifice is forbidden (Heb. 6: 6; 9: 25, 26; 10: 11, 12).

3. The Lord's Supper is not a sacrifice, but a remembrance (I Cor. 11: 26).

III. That the fruit of the vine is only to be taken by the priests (Introduced in the Council of Constance 1414).

THE BIBLE:

1. Both bread and fruit of the vine are to be given to all Christians (Matt. 26: 27; Mark 14: 23; I Cor. 11: 28).

IV. That the mass is the same sacrifice as that on the cross, only "unbloody".

THE BIBLE:

1. A bloody sacrifice is the only one known (Heb. 10: 10).

2. Only one sacrifice of Christ (Heb. 10: 12).

EXTREME UNCTION

CATHOLICISM TEACHES:

I. That this gives health and strength to the soul and

sometimes to the body when one is at the point of death.

The Bible:

1. Where is the book, chapter and verse for such a practice?

HOLY ORDERS

Catholicism Teaches:

I. That holy orders are a sacrament by which the bishop, priests and officers of the church are ordained to office.

The Bible:

1. The Scriptures are silent on such a practice.

MATRIMONY

Catholicism Teaches:

I. That the marriage bond is a sacrament and offers grace.

The Bible:

1. The Scriptures are silent on such a practice, wherein the marriage is called a sacrament.

II. That marriage must be performed by a priest.

The Bible:

1. Where was the priest at the wedding Jesus attended? (John 2: 1-11).

III. That the marriage bond is never to be broken for any cause.

The Bible:

1. Scriptures give one reason for divorce—fornication (Matt. 5: 32).

WORSHIP OF MARY

Catholicism Teaches:

I. That Mary is immaculate, the Mother of God, spouse of the Holy Spirit, Propitiary of the world and the Gate of Heaven (Introduced as church doctrine by Pope Pius IX in 1854).

THE BIBLE:

1. The Scriptures do not call her by such names.
2. If Mary's husband was the Holy Spirit, Joseph was illegally married to her.
3. The Scriptures teach that Mary was like other women, subject to their weaknesses (Luke 2: 22).
4. Jesus recognized Mary as only a human being (John 2: 3, 4).
5. Mary realized Jesus was her Saviour (Luke 1: 47).
   NOTE: The Mother of God would not need a saviour.
6. The Scriptures accord worship to the BABE and not to the mother.
7. Mary did not hold a superior position in the early church. She is only mentioned as attending a prayer meeting (Acts 1: 4).
8. Mary commands men to follow Jesus, not her (John 2: 5).

IMAGES

CATHOLICISM TEACHES:

I. That it is not unscriptural to worship images. (Introduced in the Council of Trent.)

   THE BIBLE:

   1. The use of images forbidden (Ex. 20: 4; Isa. 42: 8).

II. That they do not worship the image, but the one the image represents.

   THE BIBLE:

   1. God said we should have no graven images before Him (Ex. 20: 4).
   2. NOTE: Catholicism ascribes to different images

29

of the same personage different attributes, so they after all do make the image the object of worship.

WORSHIP OF ANGELS

CATHOLICISM TEACHES:

I. That one may pray to saints and angels. (Introduced during the sixth century.)

THE BIBLE:

1. Scriptures say the saints can not hear prayers (Eccl. 9: 6).

2. Only one mediator between man and God (John 14: 6; I Tim. 2: 5).

3. Scriptures forbid angel worship (Col. 2: 18).

4. Angels are created servants and it would be idolatry to worship them (Heb. 1: 5-13; Rev. 22: 8, 9).

SUMMARY

I. Paul saw this apostate church coming.

1. He warned the elders of Ephesus (Acts 20: 29, 30).

2. He said grievous wolves were to arise from the eldership (Acts 20: 30).

3. Grievous wolves did enter in from among ambitious elders and Peter admonished against such lording it over God's heritage (I Peter 5: 3).

4. There was a plurality of bishops or elders in each church, but no bishop or elder ever ruled over a plurality of churches until the apostacy came (Phil. 1: 1; Acts 14: 23; Titus 1: 5).

5. The apostacy came when bishops or elders were appointed over a district, archbishops over many districts, cardinals over all these and finally a pope over all. Authority was usurped in writing creeds and binding them on the consciences of men.

6. Paul said, "The Spirit speaketh expressly, that

in the latter times some shall depart from the faith, giving heed to seducing spirits and doctrines of devils. . . . forbidding to marry and commanding to abstain from meats" (I Tim. 4: 1, 3).

NOTE: The Catholic Church, teaching the doctrines of devils, forbids her priests and sisters to marry and commands the church members to abstain from meats on certain days.

II. Peter saw the same apostacy.

1. False teachers were to arise (II Peter 2: 1).

III. Jude saw the same thing and realized it was a fulfillment of all the apostles had spoken concerning the falling away (Jude 17-19).

LUTHERAN

The Lutheran Church dates from the eve of All Saints Day, Oct. 31, 1517, when Martin Luther tacked his celebrated 95 theses on the Castle Church in Wittenberg, in protest against the sale of indulgences as carried on by the Roman Church under Tetzel in Germany. Luther had no intention at the time of withdrawing from the Catholic Church, in which he was a priest or monk, but was striving to put down a great evil. However, unconsciously he had struck a great blow at the papacy and this led to the reformation and the origin of the Lutheran Church.

The Lutheran movement early divided into two branches, the Lutheran or Conservative branch and the Reformed or more radical branch. Doctrinally, their chief points of difference are the sacraments.

Lutherianism is the established church of Denmark, Norway and Sweeden. Germany is largely Lutheran. The people of Finland and a large percentage of the population of Switzerland are Lutheran. Immigration to the new world planted the Lutheran Church in America. The Lutherans in this country are divided into a number of separate bodies, formed in some instances according to the locality and in others on the basis of the language spoken in assembled worship.

THE LUTHERAN CHURCH TEACHES:

I. That the church has different branches of which the Lutheran Church is one.

"Different branches of the Christian Church draw different conclusions from the Word of God. . " (Ans. to Ques. No. 67, H. L.).

"Does it make any difference to which branch of the Christian Church one belongs?"

"Yes. Confessions are the embodiment of different faiths and of different methods of evangelizing the world; therefore it is important that we unite with that branch of the church whose confession of faith is in harmony with the Scriptures." (Ques. and Ans. No. 68, H. L.)

NOTE: Where are the trunk and limbs?

1. Trunk.
   (1.) The Lutheran Church teaches that she came from the Catholic Church.
   (2.) The Catholic Church teaches that she is the mother of all churches. (See her catechism.)

2. Other Limbs.
   (1.) The Lutheran Church teaches that she is the mother and source of the Episcopal, the Presbyterian and the Methodist Churches.

   PROOF:

   Ques. 46. "In what sense is the Lutheran Church the mother of the Episcopal Church?" (H. L.)

   Ques. 50. "Why may the Lutheran Church be considered the source of the Presbyterian Church? H. L.)

   Ques. 51. "Is the Lutheran Church the source of the Methodist Church? (H. L.)

THE BIBLE:

1. The Catholic Church as the trunk is the apostate church (II Thes. 17: 1-18).

2. The Catholic Church is called the Mother of Harlots (Rev. 17: 1-18), because:
   (1.) She is a city on seven hills (Rev. 17: 9, 18).

   NOTE: Rome, the head of the Catholic Church, rests on the seven Palatine hills.

   (2.) She sits upon many waters—peoples, mul-

titudes, nations and tongues (Rev. 17:
1, 15).

(3.) She has made the world drunk with the
wine of her spiritual fornication (Rev.
17: 1, 2).

(4.) She is drunk with the blood of the martyrs (Rev. 17: 6).

NOTE: Read the history of her inquisitions.

(5.) She is the Mother of Harlots (Rev. 17:
5).

NOTE: She herself claims to be the
mother of all churches.

3. The Scriptures say the axe is laid at the root of
the unfruitful tree to hew it down (Matt. 3:
10; Luke 3: 9).

4. Christ is the Vine and we, as individuals (not
churches) are the branches (John 15: 1-6).

THE BIBLE:

1. The Church.
   (1.) Christ built ONE church, not churches
   (Matt. 16: 18).

   (2). Christ said there is ONE fold, not folds
   (John 10: 16).

   (3.) There was ONE church set up at Pentecost (Acts 2: 47).

   (4.) Christ purchased the church, not churches
   (Acts 20: 28).

   (5.) We are ONE body in Christ (Rom. 12: 5).

   (6.) Christ is the head of the ONE body, the
   church (Col. 1: 18, 24).

2. One Faith.
   (1.) Paul said there is ONE faith (Eph. 4: 5,
   13; I Tim. 4: 1).

   (2.) Jude said there is ONE faith (Jude 3).

3. Division is unScriptural.
   (1.) Christ prayed that all might be ONE (John 17: 20-23).
   (2.) Paul denounced division (I Cor. 1: 10-13).

II. That there are three kinds of law given in the Old Testament (Civil, ceremonial and moral).
"Three kinds of law are given in the Old Testament, the civil, the ceremonial and the moral law." (Ques. and Ans. No. 18 L. S. C.)

THE BIBLE:

1. The Bible knows only one law.
(II Chron. 31: 3; Neh. 8: 2, 3, 8, 14, 18; Mal. 4: 4; Matt. 22. 36-40; Luke 24: 44.)

III. That the ten commandments are binding on us today.
"What is the moral law? Ans. "The moral law is that law which sets forth our duties to God and man, as briefly comprehended in the ten commandments." (Ques. and Ans. No. 21, L. S. C.)
"The moral law alone is binding on all men." (Ans. No. 22, L. S. C.)

THE BIBLE:

1. The ten commandments are done away (II Cor. 3: 7-11).
   NOTE: The ten commandments were "written and engraven in stones."

2. The ten commandments are called a covenant. (Ex. 34: 27, 28; Deut. 4: 12, 13; 9: 9; I Kings 8: 9, 21; II Chron. 5: 10; 6: 11.)

3. The covenant of the ten commandments is abolished (Jer. 31: 31-34; Heb. 8: 6-13; 9: 15-17).

4. Paul says it was nailed to the cross (Col. 2: 14).

5. The law was a curse and we are redeemed from the curse (Gal. 3: 13).

6. We are become dead to the law by the body of Christ (Rom. 7: 1-4).

7. Those justified by the law are fallen from grace (Gal. 5: 4).

   NOTE: If the ten commandments are binding today why do not the Lutherans keep the seventh day Sabbath, which is a part of the ten commandments (Ex. 20: 8-11).

IV. That the First day of the week is now the Sabbath.
   "By what other name is the Christian Sabbath known?"

   "The Christian Sabbath is known as the Lord's Day."

   THE BIBLE:

   1. The Sabbath is the seventh day of the week (Ex. 20: 8-11).

   2. The Lord's Day is the first day of the week (Matt. 28: 1-10; John 20: 19-29; Acts 20: 7; I Cor. 16: 1, 2; Rev. 1: 10).

V. That they should wear the name of Luther.
   "After whom was the regenerated church named?"

   "After Martin Luther, Lutheran was the name applied in derision to the evangelical Christians by the priests." (Ques. and Ans. 27, H. L.)

   "Did his followers like the name Lutheran?"

   "Yes. Some were proud of it; others adopted it because they were unwilling to repudiate the name, lest thereby they should seem to reject Luther and his doctrines." (Ques. and Ans. No. 28, H. L.)

   THE BIBLE:

   1. Adam and his wife wore the same name (Gen 5: 2).

   2. Adam was a figure of Christ (Rom. 5: 14).

3. Adam's wife is a figure of Christ's wife—the church.

4. Adam and his wife wearing the same name pictures the fact that Christ and His wife, the church, should wear the same name.

5. Prophesied that Christ's servants would be given a new name when salvation went out from Jerusalem and the Gentiles saw His righteousness (Isa. 62: 1, 2).

6. Prophecy fulfilled.

    (1.) Salvation went out from Jerusalem (Acts 2: 1-47; Luke 24: 47).

    (2.) The Gentiles saw His righteousness (Acts 10: 1-48; 11: 1).

    (3.) When these two things came to pass the new name was given—"Christian" (Acts 11: 25, 26).

    (4.) Note: "C-H-R-I-S-T-ian. The word means "belonging to Christ."

7. Agrippa knew the followers of Christ wore that name (Acts 26: 28).

8. Peter commands us to suffer in the name Christian (I Peter 4: 16).

9. We wear Christ's name in two worlds (Rev. 22: 4).

10. No salvation promised in any other name (Acts 4: 12).

Luther:

He said: "I pray you leave my name alone and not to call yourselves Lutherans, but Christians. Who is Luther? My doctrine is not mine. I have not been crucified for any one . . . How does it then benefit me, a miserable bag of dust and ashes, to give my name to the children of Christ? Cease, my dear friends, to cling to these party names and distinctions; away with all of them; and let us call ourselves only

Christians, after Him from whom our doctrine comes" (Life of Luther, by Michelet, p. 262).

VI. That the mode of baptism is non-essential.

"Lutherans hold that the mode of baptism is no essential part of the sacrament, any more than the mode of celebrating the Lord's Supper is essential to it. Neither the meaning of the word baptism, nor the occasion of its administration in the Scriptures show how the sacrament was administered. The instances referred to (Matt. 3: 7; John 3: 22, 23; 4: 1, 2; Acts 2: 41; 8: 32, 36, 38; 9: 18; 10: 47, 48; 16: 15, 33) together with the analogy of the Old Testament ordinances and expressions indicate pouring and what is called sprinkling as quite as likely, to say the least, as immersion. For those and other reasons the Lutheran Church baptizes by sprinkling or affusion." (Note under Ques. 328 L. S. C.)

THE BIBLE:

1. Christ was baptized "in" Jordan and "came up out of" the water (Mark 1: 9, 10).

2. Christ called baptism "a birth" (John 3: 5).

3. Baptism is called a "going down into" and a "coming up out of" (Acts 8: 36-39).

4. Baptism is called a washing (Acts 22: 16).

5. Baptism is called a "burial" (Rom. 6: 4).

    NOTE: The Lutherans quote this in their teaching on baptism, yet say the Scriptures does not indicate the mode.

6. Baptism is called a "planting" (Rom. 6: 5).

7. Baptism is called a "resurrection" (Col. 2: 12).

8. Baptism is called a "washing of regeneration" (Titus 3: 5).

9. The Greek word "baptizo" means to dip, plunge or immerse".

10. Only one Baptism (Eph. 4: 5).

(1.) Paul, after calling baptism a burial, a planting and a resurrection, says there is only ONE baptism. He spoke by inspiration and ought to know.

LUTHER:

He said: "First, baptism is a Greek word. In Latin it can be translated immersion, as when we plunge something into water that it may be completely covered with water."

VII. That infants should be baptized.

"Most certainly infants are to be baptized; and that on account of many and weighty reasons; but especially because:

1. "Our Lord Jesus Christ declares, 'Of such is the kingdom of God.'"

NOTES Where is there any mention of baptism in this? (Mark 10: 15) explains by saying a man must receive the kingdom as a little child.

2. "He directs us to bring them to Him; therefore we should bring them in the way appointed by Him, baptizing and teaching them" (Matt. 19: 14; 28: 19, 20).

NOTE: (1.) Jesus did not say, "bring them," but said, "suffer them to come." Where is there any reference to baptism here; and even if there were, they are to come of their own accord.

(2.) They have reversed the order in saying "baptizing and teaching them." In Matt. 28: 19, 20, it reads: "Teach all nations, baptizing them."

(3.) A child which is an infant can not be taught.

3. "As in the Old Testament children were received into the covenant of God, so also are we assured

in the New covenant, 'the promise is unto you, and to your children' " (Acts 2: 39).

NOTE: In the new covenant they were to hear (Rom. 10: 13-17), believe (Heb. 11: 6; Mark 16: 15, 16), repent (Luke 13: 3; Acts 17: 30), and be baptized (Mark 16: 15, 16; Acts 2: 38). Again the promise was to be unto "your children" "even to as many as the Lord our God shall call." The Lord calls through the Gospel (II Thes. 2: 14) and the Gospel has to be heard and obeyed. An infant can not do this.

4. "The Holy Scriptures inform us that entire families were baptized by the apostles" (Acts 16: 15, 33; I Cor. 1: 16).

NOTES Where is a child ever mentioned in this household? These households were "preached" to, showing the members were old enough to hear.

NOTE: There is no mention anywhere of a child ever being baptized. The Scriptures mention none.

NOTE: Yet in answer to (Question 264, L. S. C.) they teach each one must believe for himself. How can an infant fulfill this requirement?

LUTHER: "It can not be proved by the sacred Scriptures that infant baptism was instituted by Christ, or begun by the first Christians after the apostles."

VIII. That baptism takes the place of circumcision.

"Children were to receive circumcision, the token of the covenant which God made with Abraham, and the seal of the righteousness of faith; so now children are to be baptized, and receive the token of the new covenant, the seal of the same righteousness of faith." (Note under answer to Question 335, L. S. C.)

THE BIBLE:

1. Circumcision in the flesh was only a shadow of true circumcision, which is of the heart. (Heb. 10: 1; Rom. 2: 29.)

2. Nothing can take the place of circumcision, since real circumcision did not come in until the Christian dispensation.

IX. That the Lord's Supper is called the Sacrament of the Altar, the Lord's Supper, the Table of the Lord, the Holy Communion, and the Eucharist.

THE BIBLE:

1. The institution is called:
    (1.) The breaking of bread (Acts 2: 42; 20: 7).
    (2.) The Communion (I Cor. 10: 16).
    (3.) The Table of the Lord (I Cor. 10: 21).
    (4.) The Lord's Supper (I Cor. 11: 20, 21).

2. NOTE: The names "Sacrament of the Altar", "the Holy Communion" and the "Eucharist" are not found in the New Testament.

X. That the bread and the wine are the body and blood of Jesus Christ.

"It is the true body and blood of our Lord Jesus Christ, under the bread and the wine, instituted by Christ Himself for us to eat and to drink" (And. to Ques. No. 351, L. S. C.) "We receive the body and the blood of Christ when we partake of the sacramental bread and wine" (Ans. to Ques. No. 354, L. S. C.).

THE BIBLE:

1. Teaches that Christ was materially present "outside" of the emblems (Luke 22: 19).

2. Teaches that we are to remember Him, showing He is not materially present (I Cor. 11: 24).

3. NOTE: When Christ said, "I am the Vine," did He become a literal vine? When He said, "I am the door," did He become a literal door?

41

XI. That the Lord's Supper need not be kept each first
day of the week.

THE BIBLE:

1. Teaches that the Supper should be kept every
first day of the week (Acts 2: 42; 20: 7; I Cor.
16: 1, 2).

All quotations taken from Historical Lutheranism
(H. L.) and Luther's Short Catechism (L. S.
C.).

PRESBYTERIAN

John Calvin was born at Nayon, France, July 10, 1509. Through his study of the New Testament in the original, he gave up the Catholic Church, and became the founder of the doctrinal system known as Calvinism, which is usually associated with Presbyterianism, although there are a number of churches not Presbyterian in government that hold Calvinistic tenets. Presbyterianism, strictly speaking, refers only to that form of church government conducted under the reign of presbyters. The word Presbyterian comes from the Greek word, "presbuteros", which is translated elder, hence a Presbyterian Church is one governed by elders.

Calvin, however, never founded a distinct denomination, but he preached and put into practice the principles which underlie all Presbyterian Churches.

Presbyterianism became very powerful in Scotland under the leadership of John Knox. The first book of discipline was written in 1560, but it was not until 1592 that Parliament made Presbyterianism the established faith in Scotland. The Westminster Association, which was in session from July 1, 1643, to February 22, 1649, framed the Westminster Confession of faith, which became the doctrinal foundation of English and American Presbyterianism. Francis Makemie, who is called the "Father of American Presbyterianism", organized the Rehoboth Church in Maryland in 1684. Throughout the history of Presbyterianism there have been some seventeen distinct divisions.

Presbyterianism Teaches:

I. That "God has predestinated and fordained some men and angels out of His free grace and love without any foresight of faith or works in man or perserevance in either of them, and others are foreordained to everlasting death and the number of either is so certain and definite that it can not be increased or diminished." (West-

43

minster Confession of Faith, Art. 3, 4, 5; Chap. 3; Art. 2, Chap. 10.)

THE BIBLE:

1. Salvation is for all who believe and obey the Gospel (Matt. 28: 19, 20; Mark 16: 15, 16; John 3: 16; Acts 2: 38, 39; II Thes. 2: 14; II Peter 1: 10; 3: 9).

II. That "elect infants dying in infancy are regenerated and saved by Christ through the Spirit, so also are all other elect persons who are incapable of being outwardly called by the ministry of the Word." (Westminster Confession of Faith, Art. 3, Chap. 10.)

THE BIBLE:

1. Salvation is promised to those who believe and are baptized (Mark 16: 15, 16).

2. Without faith we can not come to God (Rom. 10: 13-17; Heb. 11: 6).

III. That faith alone will save.

THE BIBLE:

1. A man having faith without works can not be saved (James 2: 14).

2. Faith without works is dead (James 2: 17).

3. If faith alone can save, then all the devils would be saved, for they believe (James 2: 19).
   NOTE: This would be universal salvation.

4. Faith is made perfect by works (James 2: 22).

5. We are not justified by faith only (James 2: 24).

6. Faith without works is dead as the body without the Spirit (James 2: 26).

7. Faith only gives us "power to become" sons of God (John 1: 12).

IV. That confession to the apostles' creed is necessary.

1. The only creed of Christianity is a living personality, Christ (Matt. 16: 16).
2. The Church is built upon the confession of Christ as the Son of God (Matt. 16: 18).
3. This is the only confession required (Acts 8: 36-39; Rom. 10: 10; Matt. 10: 32, 33; I John 4: 2).

V. That there are three baptisms—sprinkling, pouring, immersion.

THE BIBLE:

1. The practice of the apostles and the early church was immersion.
2. Baptism is called:
   (1.) A "birth" (John 3: 5).
   (2.) A "going down into" and a "coming up out of" (Acts 8: 36-39).
   (3.) A "washing" (Acts 22: 16).
   (4.) A "burial" (Rom. 6: 4).
   (5.) A "planting" (Rom. 6: 5).
   (6.) A "resurrection" (Col. 2: 12).
   (7.) A "cleansing" (Eph. 5: 26).
   (8.) A "washing of the body" (Heb. 10: 22).
   (9.) A "washing of regeneration" (Titus 3: 5).
   (10.) There is ONE baptism (Eph. 4: 5).

VI. That the Church should practice infant baptism. (Vote of the Westminster Assembly, which was in session from July 1, 1643, to February 22, 1649. The vote was twenty-four to retain sprinkling and twenty-five to drop dipping.)

THE BIBLE:

1. Without faith it is impossible to come to God (Heb. 11: 6).
2. Faith cometh by hearing (Rom. 10: 17).
3. He that believeth and is baptized shall be saved (Mark 16: 16).

NOTE: An infant can not comply with either requirement and therefore is not a proper subject of baptism.

4. There is not one mention of a child ever being baptized. The household converts were preached to, showing they were old enough to hear.

VII. That there is no salvation in a name.

THE BIBLE:

1. Adam and his wife wore the same name (Gen. 5: 2).

2. Adam was a figure of Christ (Rom. 5: 14).

3. Adam's wife is a figure of Christ's wife, the Church.

4. Adam and his wife wearing the same name pictures the fact that Christ and His wife, the Church, should wear the same name.

5. Prophesied that Christ's servants should be given a new name when salvation went out from Jerusalem and the Gentiles saw His righteousness (Isa. 62: 1, 2).

6. Prophecy fulfilled.

   (1.) Salvation went out from Jerusalem (Acts 2: 1-47; Luke 24: 47).

   (2.) The Gentiles saw His righteousness (Acts 10: 1-48; Acts 11: 1).

   (3.) When these two things came to pass the new name was given—Christian (Acts 11: 25, 26).

   (4.) NOTE: "Christ-ian" means belonging to Christ.

7. Agrippa knew the followers of Christ wore that name (Acts 26: 28).

8. Peter commanded us to suffer in the name "Christian" (I Peter 4: 16).

9. We wear Christ's name in two worlds (Rev. 22: 4).

46

10. No salvation promised in any other name (Acts 4: 12).

VIII. That the Lord's Supper does not need to be observed weekly.

THE BIBLE:

1. Pictured in the Old Testament that as the priests ate the shewbread once each week, we should eat the Lord's Supper once a week (Lev. 24: 5-9).

NOTE: The things under the law were a shadow of good things to come (Heb. 10: 1).

2. The early church continued steadfastly in the breaking of bread (Acts 2: 42).

3. The early church communed every first day (Acts 20: 7).

NOTE: Same phraseology as found in (I Cor. 16: 1, 2) and all understand that the collection is to be taken every week.

4. There is no life in us if we do not commune (John 6: 53).

NOTE: Calvin said: "And truly this custom, which enjoins communing once a year, is a most wicked contrivance of the devil, by whose instrumentality soever it may have been determined." (Institutes Book 4, Chap. 17.)

"It ought to have been far otherwise. Every week at least the table of the Lord should have been spread for Christian assemblies, and the promises declared by which in partaking of it, we might be spiritually fed." (Institutes Book 6, Chap. 18.)

IX. That the Holy Spirit acts directly upon the heart of a man to persuade him to obey the call of the Gospel.

"We believe in the Holy Spirit, the Lord and Giver of Life, who moves everywhere upon the hearts of men to restrain them from evil and to

47

incite them to good, and whom the Father is ever willing to give unto all who ask Him. . . . and to persuade and enable them to obey the call of the Gospel." (Brief statement of the Reformed Faith for the better understanding of our doctrinal beliefs, General Assambly in Los Angeles, Cal., 1903.)

THE BIBLE:

1. Christ has promised to pray for the Holy Spirit to come to the obedient (John 14: 15-17).
2. The Holy Spirit is promised to those who repent and are baptized (Acts 2: 38).
   The Holy Spirit does not act on the unbaptized to convert them, but comes to the baptized.
3. The Holy Spirit does not act upon the man to be converted, but selects preachers to preach and the field of labor each is to preach in (Acts 8: 26-39).

X. That we are baptized in the Holy Spirit.

THE BIBLE:

1. The baptism of the Holy Spirit promised and given to the apostles (Matt. 3: 11; Acts 1: 1-5; 2: 1-4).
2. The House of Cornelius received the baptism of the Holy Spirit to prove to the Jew that the Gentile was an accepted people (Acts 10: 47, 11: 15).
3. The baptism of the Holy Spirit gives one power to perform ten kinds of miracles (Acts 2: 4-12; 5: 12-16; 9: 36-42; 20: 8-10).
   NOTE: These were signs of an apostle (II Cor. 12: 12).
4. If a man claims to be baptized in the Holy Spirit today, then the world has a right to demand of him the working of miracles.
5. The baptism of the Holy Spirit came with a rushing mighty wind and cloven tongues as of fire (Acts 2: 1-4).

48

NOTE: None receives such a manifestation today.

XI. That the ten commandments are binding on men today.

"We believe that the law of God, revealed in the ten commandments, and more clearly disclosed in the words of Christ, is forever established in truth and equity, so that no human work shall abide except it be built on this foundation." (Art. 13, 1903 Assembly.)

THE BIBLE:

1. The law was given only to the Jew (Ex. 20: 1-17; Deut. 4: 8; 5: 1; Mal. 4: 4; Rom. 2: 14).

2. The ten commandments done away (II Cor. 3: 7-11).

NOTE: The part "written and engraven on stones" was the ten commandments.

3. The ten commandments are called a covenant (Ex. 34: 27, 28; Deut. 4: 12, 13; 9: 9; I Kings 8: 9, 21; II Chron. 5: 10; 6: 11).

4. The covenant of the ten commandments is abolished (Jer. 31: 31-34; Zech 11: 10-14; Heb. 8: 6-13; Heb. 9: 15-17).

5. The law was a curse and we are redeemed from the curse (Gal. 3: 13).

6. Those that are justified by the law are fallen from grace (Eph. 5: 4).

XII. That the Church should be governed by presbyters.

THE BIBLE:

1. The form of government in the beginning was congregational with elders and deacons of the local congregation (Acts 14: 23; Phil. 1: 1; I Tim. 3: 1-7).

2. There was a plurality of elders over the local congregation, but never an elder over a plurality of congregations (Phil. 1: 1; Titus 1: 5; Acts 14: 23).

3. Paul prophesied that the apostacy would arise among the elders, or bishops (Acts 20: 29, 30). NOTE: The first departure from the primitive order was when an elder or bishop began to oversee more than one church, then a district. This finally produced a pope sitting at Rome claiming authority over the entire Church.

4. Peter saw the danger of ambitious elders lording it over God's heritage (I Peter 5: 3).

EPISCOPALIAN

The Episcopal Church was originated by Henry VIII after his quarrel with the Catholic Church because the pope of Rome refused to annul his marriage to Catherine of Aragon, that he might be free to marry Anne Boleyn, an Irish beauty with whom he became infatuated. Through the conniving of Henry, the English Parliament was induced to sever the connection of the Church of England and the Church of Rome and make him head of the English Church.

During the reign of Henry VIII, Thomas Cranmer began the writing of the Book of Homilies and the Forty-Two Articles. Later this book was reduced to Thirty-Nine Articles as now incorporated in the Common Book of Prayer. The Episcopal Church of today is based upon the Apostles' and Nicene Creeds, together with the Thirty-Nine Articles of the Church of England.

The Church of England was established in the new world by English colonists and was under the jurisdiction of the Bishop of London. This ecclesiastical connection was severed during the War of the Revolution and the Church of England in the colonies became the Protestant Episcopal Church in the United States. The Episcopal Church derives its name from its Episcopalian form of government inherited from the Roman Church whereby the churches are governed by bishops or overseers. The word overseer comes from the Greek word, "episkopos", hence the name, Episcopal.

EPISCOPALIANISM TEACHES:

I. That the Church should be governed by the episcopacy.

THE BIBLE:

1. No such thing as Diocesan Episcopacy—one bishop ruling over several churches—to be found in the New Testament.

2. Bishop and elder are two names for the same officer in the New Testament (Acts 20: 17, 28; Titus 1: 5-7; I Peter 5: 1-3),

3. Each New Testament congregation had a plurality of bishops or elders, but there is no case of a bishop or elder being over a plurality of churches (Acts 14: 23; 15: 2, 22, 23; 16: 4; Phil. 1: 1, 2; I Tim. 3: 1-7; I Tim. 5: 17).

II. That their bishops are successors to the apostles.

THE BIBLE:

1. An apostle is a witness (Luke 1: 2; 24: 33; Acts 1: 1-3, 19-22; Acts 10: 39-41; I Cor. 9: 1; 15: 5, 7, 8; II Peter 1: 16; I John 1: 1).

2. A witness can not have a successor, but another witness can testify.

3. Only one case of apostolic succession in the Scriptures (Acts 1: 15-26).

4. A successor of an apostle must have companied with Christ from the baptism of John to the ascension of Christ (Acts 1: 21, 22).

5. None today, or immediately following the days of the apostles could meet the requirements of an apostle or the successor to an apostle. Therefore apostolic succession is unScriptural.

6. When James was beheaded they did not meet and select one to take his place as in the case of Judas (Acts 2: 15-26; 15: 1-29).

7. Modern episcopacy is popery with the pope omitted.

III. That the Church has a priesthood, based upon the continuation of the Aaronic priesthood.

THE BIBLE:

1. No priesthood in the New Testament except that of Jesus Christ as the High Priest (Heb. 7: 12-15).

2. And the Priesthood of all believers (I Peter 2: 5).

3. The Aaronic priesthood superseded by a greater priesthood, that of Christ, which is after the order of Melchizedek (Heb. 7: 11-17).

4. Christ is the **High Priest and His body of obedient believers the priesthood** (Heb. 4: 15; I Peter 2: 5, 9; Rev. 1: 5, 6).

5. No authority given to the Christian ministry—only commissioned to teach and preach (Matt. 28: 18, 19).
   Christ has all authority (Matt. 28: 18).

IV. That the authority of the Church is to be found in the canon law and prayer book rubrics.

THE BIBLE:

1. The Bible alone is sufficient (Isa. 8: 20; Matt. 28: 18; John 12: 48; Rev. 22: 18, 19).

V. That Christ died to reconcile His Father to us.
   "Who suffered, was crucified, dead and buried to reconcile His Father to us." (Art. 2, Prayer Book.)

THE BIBLE:

1. The exact opposite is true—Christ was in the world to reconcile us to the Father (II Cor. 5: 18, 19: Rom. 5: 10).

VI. That we are justified by faith only.
   "Wherefore that we are justified by faith only is a most wholesome doctrine and very full of comfort." (Art. 11, Prayer Book.)

THE BIBLE:

1. Faith without works is dead (James 2: 17).

2. Faith without works is as dead as the body without the spirit (James 2: 26).

3. If faith alone will save, all the devils will be saved, for they believe (James 2: 19).
   NOTE: This would be universal salvation.

4. Justification is by works and NOT by Faith ONLY (James 2: 24).

5. Faith only gives us power to become sons of God (John 1: 12).

6. We are justified by:
   (1.) By God (Rom. 8: 33).
   (2.) By Christ (Acts 13: 39).
   (3.) By Faith (Rom. 5: 1).
   (4.) By Christ's blood (Rom. 5: 9).
   (5.) By the name of Jesus (I Cor. 6: 11).
   (6.) By grace (Titus 3: 7).
   (7.) By works (James 2: 24).

VII. That the Lord's Supper is a sacrifice or mass.

THE BIBLE:
1. The Lord's Supper is a memorial of a "finished" sacrifice (Luke 22: 19; I Cor. 11: 24).
2. The Lord's Supper is a communion (I Cor. 10: 16).
3. Christ was only sacrificed once (Heb. 7: 27; Heb. 6: 6; Heb. 9: 12, 24-28; 10: 11, 12).

VIII. That the worship of the congregation is to be governed by the ritual.

THE BIBLE:
1. New Testament church had no prayer book.

IX. That affusion is sufficient for baptism.

THE BIBLE:
1. Baptism is a birth (John 3: 5).
2. Baptism is a "going down into" and a "coming up out of" (Acts 8: 36-39).
3. Baptism is a washing (Acts 22: 16).
4. Baptism is a burial (Rom. 6: 4).
5. Baptism is a planting (Rom. 6: 5).
6. Baptism is a resurrection (Col. 2: 12).
7. There is only ONE baptism (Eph. 4: 5).

   NOTE: The Church of England practiced immersion until after the reformation. The second prayer book of Edward VI gave permission to practice affusion. The Rubric in the English Church and in the Protestant Episcopal

54

Church now reads: "They shall be dipped."
Episcopalians do not follow their own rubric,
but rather Roman Catholicism.

X. That the infant is regenerated in baptism.

"Almighty and immortal God, the aid of all who
need, the helper of all who flee to Thee for suc-
cor, the life of those who believe and the resurrection of the dead; we call upon Thee for this
infant, that he, coming to thy holy baptism, may
receive remission of sins, by spiritual regeneration. Receive him, O Lord, as thou hast promised by thy well beloved Son. (Book of Common Prayer, p. 230.)

THE BIBLE:

1. One must hear, believe, repent, confess Christ
and be baptized (Rom. 10: 13-17; Heb. 11: 6;
Luke 13: 3; Acts 17: 30; II Peter 3: 9; Matt.
10: 32; Acts 8: 37; Mark 16: 15, 16).

2. NOTE: "In the apostolic age and in the three
centuries which followed it, it is evident that, as
a general rule, those who came to baptism, came
in full age, of their own deliberate choice . . . .
the old liturgical service of baptism was framed
for full-grown converts and is only by adapta-
tion applied to the case of infants." (Christian
Institutions, pp. 19, 20. Arthur P. Stanley,
Dean of Westminster Abbey and leading scholar
of the Church of England.)

XI. That there is no salvation in a name.

THE BIBLE:

1. Adam and his wife wore the same name (Gen.
5: 2).

2. Adam is a figure of Christ (Rom. 5: 14).

3. Adam's wife is then a figure of Christ's wife,
the Church.

4. Adam and his wife wearing the same name pic-

tured Christ and His wife, the church, wearing the same name.

5. Phophesied that a new name was to be given by the mouth of the Lord when salvation went out from Jerusalem and the Gentiles saw His righteousness.

6. The prophecy fulfilled.
   (1.) Salvation went out from Jerusalem (Acts 2: 1-47; Luke 24: 47).
   (2.) The Gentiles saw His righteousness (Acts 10: 1-48; 11: 1).
   (3.) The New name given—Christian (Acts 11: 25, 26).

7. We are married to Christ and should wear His name (Rom. 7: 4).

8. King Agrippa knew the followers of Christ wore the name Christian (Acts 26: 28).

9. The Holy Spirit, through Peter, commanded us to suffer in the name Christian (I Peter 4: 16).

10. There is no salvation in any other name (Acts 4: 12).

METHODIST

Methodism was founded by John Wesley, an ordained priest in the Episcopal Church. Wesley lived and died an Episcopalian and had no intention of organizing a new church. The Methodist Episcopal Church came into existence in this manner: John and Charles Wesley, with Whitefield and about a dozen other students at Oxford formed themselves into a society for the purpose of overcoming the formalism and ritualism of the Episcopal Church and to stimulate piety and spirituality among its members. Other societies were organized and because of their methodical manner of life they were called Methodists. The appellation obtained currency and upon the death of Wesley these societies banded together under a conference and became known as the Methodist Episcopal Church, although they for a time considered themselves a part of the Episcopal Church.

The Methodist Episcopal Church of the United States originated with the Christian Conference held in Baltimore, Dec. 24, 1784. The Baltimore conference adopted the Book of Discipline prepared by Wesley which reduced the thirty-nine articles of the Episcopal Prayer Book to twenty-four articles and added one covering the rulers of the United States. Also the Apostles' Creed, which the Episcopal Church inherited from the Roman Catholic Church, was incorporated in their form of worship.

The English Church is divided into some nine subdivisions, while the American Methodists are divided into over fifteen separate bodies.

THE METHODIST CHURCH TEACHES:

I. That the Church is composed of many branches, of which the Methodist Church is one. (Preamble of the Constitution of the Methodist Episcopal Church.)

THE BIBLE:

1. Christ established only one church (Matt. 16:

18; Acts 20: 28; Rom. 12: 4, 5; I Cor. 10: 17; Col. 1: 18; I Cor. 12: 13).

2. NOTE: If the Methodist Church is one of the branches, where are the trunk and limbs?

(1.) The Episcopal Church is the mother of the Methodist Church.

(2.) The Catholic Church is the mother of the Episcopal Church.

(3.) Therefore the Catholic Church is the trunk and the denominations which came from her are the branches.

(4.) The Catholic Church is called the Mother of Harlots in the Scriptures (Rev. 17: 1-18).

  a. She is a city on seven hills (Rev. 17: 9, 18).
     NOTE: Rome is built on seven hills.

  b. She sits on many waters—peoples, multitudes, nations and tongues (Rev. 17: 1, 15).

  c. She has made the world drunk with the wine of her spiritual fornication (Rev. 17: 1, 2).

  d. She is drunk with the blood of martyrs (Rev. 17: 6).
     NOTE: Read the history of her inquisitions.

  e. She is the Mother of "Harlots" (Rev. 17: 5).
     NOTE: In her catechism she teaches she is the mother of all churches.

(5.) The Scriptures say that the axe is laid at the root of the unfruitful tree to hew it down (Matt. 3: 10; Luke 3: 9).

(6.) Christ is the Vine and we, as individuals (not churches) are the branches (John 15: 1-6).

II. That division is permissible and even advisable.

THE BIBLE:

1. One way, not ways, prophesied (Job 28: 7; Isa. 35: 8).
2. Christ said there is one way (Matt. 7: 13, 14; John 14: 6).
3. Christ said there is one fold (John 10: 1, 16).
4. Paul denounced division (I Cor. 1: 10).
5. Christ prayed for his followers to be one (John 17: 20, 21).

III. That it makes no difference what name the church members wear.

THE BIBLE:

1. Adam and his wife wore the same name (Gen. 5: 2).
2. Adam is a figure of Christ (Rom. 5: 14).
3. Adam and his wife wearing the same name pictures Christ and his wife, the Church, wearing the same name.
4. The new name prophesied to be given when salvation went out from Jerusalem and the Gentiles saw His righteousness (Isa. 62: 1, 2).
5. The new name given as prophesied (Acts 2: 1-47; 10: 1-48; 11: 1, 25, 26).
6. King Agrippa knew they wore the name "Christian" (Acts 26: 28).
7. Peter said we are to suffer in the name Christian (I Peter 4: 16).
8. No salvation promised in any other name (Acts 4: 12).

IV. That the Church is to be governed by a general conference which has full power to make rules and regulations for the church. (Art. 46, Book of Discipline.)

THE BIBLE:

1. New Testament Church was purely congrega-

tional in its form of government. No episcopacy known.

(1.) There was a plurality of elders over the local congregation, but never an elder, or bishop over a plurality of churches (Acts 14: 23; Phil. 1: 1; Titus 1: 5).

(2.) It is not the duty of the Church to make laws, but to OBEY the laws made by the Head of the Church (Col. 1: 18, 24; Matt. 28: 18).

V. That the officers of the Church are Presiding Elders, circuit riders, class leaders, stewarts, etc.

THE BIBLE:

1. Only two classes of church officers in the New Testament Church and they were only over the one local congregation (Phil. 1: 1; I Tim. 3: 8; James 5: 14).

VI. That none should be admitted into full membership of the church until he has been at least six months on probation. (Art. 49, Methodist Book of Discipline, also Art. 445.)

THE BIBLE:

1. Baptism brings a man into Christ and into the Church (Acts 2: 41, 47; Gal. 3: 27; I Cor. 12: 13).

2. They were baptized the same day they heard the Gospel, so we see they did not practice probation (Acts 8: 26-39; Acts 10: 1-48; Acts 16: 14, 15; Acts 16: 25-33; Acts 22: 11-16).

NOTE: They were baptized, thereby becoming members of the Church, the same day, even to the same hour of the night.

3. Probation is a borrowing from heathenism. Buddha, who was a heathen, put his followers on a four months' probation.

VII. That a man is justified by faith only.

"Wherefore, that we are justified by faith only, is a most wholesome doctrine, and very full of comfort." (Art. 9, Book of Discipline.)

THE BIBLE:

1. A man without works though he has faith can not be saved (James 2: 14).
2. Faith without works is dead (James 2: 17).
3. If faith alone could save, then all the devils would be saved, for they believe (James 2: 19).

NOTE: Universal salvation.

4. Faith is made perfect by works (James 2: 22).
5. We are not justified by faith "only" (James 2: 24).
6. Faith without works is as dead as the body without the spirit (James 2: 26).
7. Faith only gives us "power to become" sons of God (John 1: 12).

VIII. That man has no free will to do good without the grace of God by Christ preventing him. (Art. 8, Book of Discipline).

THE BIBLE:

1. God made man a free moral agent (Gen. 1-6).
2. "Whosoever" opens the door to all them that obey the Gospel (John 3: 16; Rev. 22: 17).
3. All men must repent or be damned (II Peter 3: 9).

IX. That salvation is offered in both the Old and New Testaments. (Art. 6, Book of Discipline).

THE BIBLE:

1. Those in Old Testament times only looked for a Saviour (Isa. 7: 14; John 9: 56; Heb. 11: 13).
2. None were saved before Christ (John 1: 17; John 3: 13; Rom. 3: 9; 11: 32; Gal. 3: 27; 3: 8, 13, 14; Eph. 2: 11, 12; I Peter 2: 9, 10).

3. The best produced before Christ was less than the least in the kingdom (Matt. 11: 11).

X. That baptism is not essential to salvation.

THE BIBLE:

We are baptized:

1. To flee the wrath to come (Matt. 3: 7).
2. To fulfill all righteousness (Matt. 3: 15).
3. To accept the counsel of God (Luke 7: 30).
4. To enter into the kingdom of God (John 3: 5).
5. To have sins remitted (Acts 2: 38).
6. To receive the Holy Spirit (Acts 2: 38).
7. To get into the church (I Cor. 12: 13).
8. To get into Christ (Gal. 3: 27).
9. To save us (I Peter 3: 21).
   NOTE: Peter wrote as directed by the Holy Spirit and he said baptism saves us. To deny this is denying the Holy Spirit and calling Him a liar.
10. Christ said, "He that believeth and is baptized shall be saved" (Mark 16: 15, 16).

XI. That although baptism is not essential to salvation, they base the salvation of infants on baptism (Art. 17).
   NOTE: This is water regeneration, pure and simple.

THE BIBLE:

1. The Bible requires more than baptism.
   (1.) Faith (Heb. 11: 6; Mark 16: 15, 16).
   (2.) Repentance (Luke 13: 3; Acts 17: 30; II Peter 3: 9).
   (3.) Confession (Matt 10: 32; 16: 16; Rom. 10: 10; Acts 8: 37).
   (4.) Adding the Christian graces (Acts 2: 42; II Peter 1: 5-11).
   NOTE: No infant can do these things.

XII. That it is Scriptural to baptize unbelievers. (Art. 17, Book of Discipline.)

THE BIBLE:

1. The Gospel must be heard, believed and obeyed (Rom. 10: 13-17; Heb. 11: 6; Mark 16: 15, 16).
2. An infant, then, is not a proper subject of baptism.

XIII. That baptism takes the place of circumcision.

THE BIBLE:

1. Circumcision of the flesh is a picture of the true circumcision—that of the heart (Heb. 10: 1; Rom. 2: 29).
2. NOTE: The true circumcision did not come in until the Gospel dispensation; therefore nothing could take its place.

XIV. That there are three ways of baptizing—sprinkling, pouring and immersion (Articles 442, 444, Book of Discipline.)

THE BIBLE:

1. Only ONE baptism (Eph. 4: 5).
2. Baptism is:
   (1.) A birth (John 3: 5).
   (2.) A going down into and a coming up out of (Acts 8: 36-39).
   (3.) A washing (Acts 22: 16).
   (4.) A burial (Rom. 6: 4; Col. 2: 12).
   (5.) A planting (Rom. 6: 5).
   (6.) A resurrection (Col. 2: 12).

XV. That the Holy Spirit works on sinners to save them.

THE BIBLE:

1. Holy Spirit arranged fields of labor for ministers (Acts 8: 26-35).

2. Holy Spirit selects and sends preachers (Acts 8: 26-35; 13: 2).

NOTE: The Holy Spirit never acts directly on the sinner.

3. Christ alone has the right to pray for the Holy Spirit to be given (John 14: 15-17).

XVI. That those who are baptized in water may also be baptized in the Holy Spirit. (Articles 442, 443, Book of Discipline.)

THE BIBLE:

1. The Holy Spirit operates in three degrees.

(1.) Baptismal (Acts 2: 1-4; Acts 10: 44-48).

(2.) Laying on of hands of an apostle (Acts 8: 12-17; 19: 6; II Tim. 1: 6).

(3.) General gift as a comforter or counselor (Acts 2: 38).

NOTE: The first gift conferred power to perform all kinds of miracles, even to the raising of the dead; the second conferred power to perform a few miracles; the last conferred no such miraculous powers.

2. Holy Spirit baptism came with a rushing of wind and tongues like as of fire (Acts 2: 1-4).

NOTE: (1.) None receive this manifestation today.

(2.) The indwelling of the Holy Spirit promised only to the obedient (I Cor. 3: 16).

XVII. That the Lord's Supper is a sacrament. (Art. 16, Book of Discipline.)

THE BIBLE:

1. The word sacrament is never found in the New Testament.

2. The word sacrament means "an oath". The Lord's Supper is not an oath.

3. The Lord's Supper is called in the New Testament:

(1.) The Breaking of Bread (Acts 2: 42; Acts 20: 7).

(2.) The Communion (I Cor. 10: 16).

(3.) The Lord's Supper (I Cor. 11: 20).

(4.) The Lord's Table (I Cor. 10: 21).

XVIII. That no person should be admitted to the Lord's Table who is guilty of any practice worthy of exclusion as a member. (Art. 446, Book of Discipline.)

THE BIBLE:

1. The test is the manner of partaking and not the worthiness of the one partaking (I Cor. 11: 28).

2. The more unworthy one is the more needful to partake, for to have life one must partake (John 6: 53).

XIX. That it is not necessary to observe the Lord's Supper each week. The Methodists commune once each quarter.

THE BIBLE:

1. The priests under the law eating the shewbread once each week pictured the priests in the Church (I Peter 2: 5, 9; Rev. 1: 6) communing each week (Lev. 24: 5-9; Heb. 10: 1).

2. The early church communed each week (Acts 20: 7).

NOTE: This is the same phraseology as (I Cor. 16: 1, 2) and all understand this to mean taking the offering each week.

3. Christ said there is no life in us if we do not partake (John 6: 53).

4. The early church continued steadfastly (Acts 2: 42).

XX. That the Church should pass upon the reception or expulsion of members. (Articles 445, 249, 250.)

THE BIBLE:

1. Christ is the only Judge (John 5: 22).
2. Christ commands us not to judge (Matt. 7: 1).
3. God adds to the Church, not man (Acts 2: 47).
4. Christ commands that the good and bad "in the kingdom" be permitted to grow together until the harvest—the end of the world (Matt. 13: 24-30, 39).

   NOTE: How many times has the spectacle been witnessed of the Church voting out bad members—the tares, and good members, friends or relatives—the wheat going out with the bad out of sympathy. Thus is rooted up the wheat with the tares.

XXI. That the Church should be governed by a discipline and its members should adhere to a creed. (Articles 69 and 442, Book of Discipline.)

NOTE: The Apostles' Creed, which is used by the Methodist Church, was never written by the apostles. The earliest record of the Apostles' Creed is found in 180 A. D., being quoted by Irenæus and the present Apostles' Creed is much larger and changed in 16 different places.

THE BIBLE:

1. The Bible is the only rule of faith and practice (Isa. 8: 20; Rev. 22: 18, 19).
2. Christ is the only creed of Christianity (Matt. 16: 16, 18; Acts 8: 37).

   NOTE: The Methodist creed is a human creed, written by human beings and is subject to change, showing how human it is

XXII. That it is permissible to use the mourners' bench.

THE BIBLE:

1. The mourners' bench is unknown in the Bible.
2. The idea of the mourner's bench is that the man must seek God, whereas God is anxious for men to be saved.

66

XXIII. That Christ was in the world to reconcile His Father to us. (Art. 2, Book of Discipline.)

THE BIBLE:

1. The exact opposite is true. Christ was in the world to reconcile the world to God (II Cor. 5: 18. 19; Rom. 5: 10).

XXIV. That a death-bed repentance will save a man.

THE BIBLE:

1. Not a case of a death-bed repentance in the Bible.

2. No salvation for the man who has not been born of the water and of the Spirit, for he is not in the kingdom (John 3: 5).

BAPTIST

The origin of the Baptist Church is hidden in obscurity, Baptists themselves being divided on the question. The first Baptist Church that is known to have existed was organized in Holland by John Smyth. Infant baptism was rejected and the position taken that a Scriptural church should be composed of those baptized on a personal confession of faith. Smyth re-baptized himself and others by affusion.

The first Baptist Church in England was organized by Thomas Helwys in 1611. They were called General Baptists. The Particular Baptists originated in 1633 and began the practice of immersion in 1641. They suffered many persecutions and were nick-named "Anabaptists" and "Cantabaptists". In 1689 the act of Toleration passed by Parliament gave them religious liberty.

The Baptists in America are not directly descended from their English brethren, having been organized by Roger Williams and Ezekiel Holliman at what is now Providence, R. I. Throughout their history the Baptists have divided into not less than twelve divisions.

While the Baptists today, generally speaking, have no confession of faith and are congregational in their form of government, in their earlier history they followed human creeds and required each congregation to subscribe to them. A confession of faith was written in London in 1677 and was accepted by the Particular Baptists in 1689. American Baptists also adopted it in Philadelphia, Pa., in 1742, and it was from that time known as the Philadelphia Confession of Faith. It is Calvinistic in its teachings. In 1833 J. Newton Brown, of New Hampshire, wrote a confession which was adopted by the New Hampshire Conference and is known as the New Hampshire Confession of Faith. It is only mildly Calvinistic. This is the most popular confession among Baptists.

THE BAPTIST CHURCH TEACHES:

I. That John the Baptist founded the Church.

THE BIBLE:

1. John's death recorded (Matt. 14: 10-12).
2. Christ promised to build His Church AFTER John was already dead and buried (Matt. 16: 18).

   NOTE: The time represented in (Matt. 16: 18) is a later date than that in (Matt. 14: 10-12) because between these two references are recorded, in the order of events, the feeding of the five thousand, Christ's walking on the sea, the healing of the Syrophenician's daughter and the feeding of the four thousand.
3. Christ at this later date promised: "I *will* build my church," showing that it was not yet built.
4. John, then, could not be a member of the Church to say nothing of being its founder.
5. Christ said that although there had not been born of women one greater than John, yet the least in the kingdom, or the Church, is greater than John (Matt. 11: 11).
6. John's disciples even had to be rebaptized after Christian baptism came into force (Acts 19: 1-5).
7. John is only the friend, not the bridegroom (John 3: 29).

II. That faith alone will save a man.

   THE BIBLE:

1. Faith without works is dead (James 2: 17).
2. Faith is shown by works (James 2: 18).
3. Faith alone classes us with the devils (James 2: 19).

   NOTE: If faith alone saves, then every devil will be saved and that would be universal salvation.
4. Faith is made perfect by works (James 2: 22).
5. A man is not saved by faith "only" (James 2: 24).

6. Faith without works is as dead as the body without the spirit (James 2: 26).

7. Some quote passages from Paul's epistles where he says no man is justified by works, but in those cases Paul is talking about the works of the law.

III. That repentance comes before faith (Mark 1: 15).

1. Looks as if the Baptists are right in this.

2. Definition of the Gospel (I Cor. 15: 1-4).

NOTE: The facts of the Gospel being the death, burial and resurrection of Christ, then the people before the cross could not believe the Gospel in its fullness. Therefore, before the cross they were told to repent and believe the Gospel —when it came.

3. Since the cross, belief comes first and repentance afterward (Heb. 11: 6).

NOTE: While repentance is mentioned first in Acts 2: 38, yet faith was not commanded first, because they already believed enough to cry out, "Men and brethren, what shall we do?"

4. We are commanded to rightly divide the Word of truth (II Tim. 2: 15). Commands before the cross were different from those after the cross.

IV. That we are to confess that we believe God for Jesus Christ's sake has forgiven us of our sins, even before we are baptized.

THE BIBLE:

1. The confession required is found in (Matt. 16: 18).

2. Christ commands us to confess Him (Matt. 10: 32).

3. Four reasons for confessing:

(1.) That Christ may confess us before the Father (Matt. 10: 32).

70

(2.) For the preacher's information (Acts 8: 36-39).

(3.) For the confessor's salvation (Rom. 10: 10).

(4.) For God's glorification (Phil 2: 9-11).

4. Baptism is "for the remission of sins" (Acts 2: 38). Therefore if we confess before baptism that God has forgiven us of our sins for Jesus Christ's sake, we are confessing to something unScriptural. Remission of sins *follows* baptism.

V. That baptism is not essential to salvation.

THE BIBLE:

1. Baptism is to flee the wrath of God (Matt. 3: 7).

2. Baptism is to fulfill all righteousness (Matt. 3: 15).

3. Christ said we must believe and be baptized to be saved (Mark 16: 15, 16).

4. Christ said under an oath, "Except a man be born of the water and the Spirit he can not enter the kingdom of God" (John 3: 5).

NOTE: Some argue that the water here refers to the natural birth. This can not be the natural birth, for Christ said we must be born "again". If this refers to natural birth, then the Baptists must admit infants into membership.

5. Baptism is for the remission of sins (Acts 2: 38).

6. Paul says we must be baptized to get into Christ (Gal. 3: 27).

NOTE: If we can be saved without baptism, then we can be saved without a Saviour, for baptism puts us into Christ.

7. Peter says baptism saves us (I Peter 3: 21).

8. Some wise ones back there thought they didn't need to be baptized (Luke 7: 30), but they

rejected the counsel of God in refusing to be baptized.

VI. That we can not fall from grace.

THE BIBLE:

1. Willful sin causes us to fall (Heb. 10: 26).

2. Paul says those who fall away can not be renewed to repentance, showing we can fall away (Heb. 6: 1-6).

3. Baptists teach we are under the law and Paul says those under the law are fallen from grace (Gal. 5: 4).

4. Paul saw the danger of falling away (I Cor. 9: 27).

VII. That there is no salvation in a name.

THE BIBLE:

1. Paul baptizing in a name made all the difference between John's baptism and Christian baptism (Acts 19: 5).

2. It is pictured that Christ and the Church should wear the same name.

(1.) Adam and his wife wore the same name (Gen. 5: 2).

(2.) Adam was a figure of Christ (Rom. 5: 14).

(3.) If Adam was a figure of Christ, Adam's wife was a figure of Christ's wife, the Church.

(4.) Adam and his wife wearing the same name pictured Christ and His wife—the Church —wearing the same name.

(5.) Prophesied that a new name should be given when salvation went out from Jerusalem and the Gentiles saw His righteousness (Isa. 62: 1, 2).

(6.) The prophecy fulfilled (Acts 2: 1-27).

1. Salvation went out from Jerusalem (Acts 2: 1-47; Luke 24: 47).

2. The Gentiles saw Christ's righteousness beginning at Cornelius' house (Acts 10: 1-48; Acts 11: 1).

3. When both parts of this prophecy was fulfilled, immediately the new name was given (Acts 11: 25, 26).

4. That is why they were called Christians "first" in Antioch.

(7.) The name, Christian, is a "new name". "Disciples", "Saints", "brethren", etc., are not new names, for they were in use among the Israelites.

(8.) Non-church members knew Christ's folfollowers wore the name, "Christian" (Acts 26: 28).

(9.) Peter commands us to suffer in the name, "Christian" (I Peter 4: 16).

(10.) Christ's name is worn in two worlds (Rev. 22: 4).

(11.) We are married to Christ and should wear His name, not the name of the bridegroom's friend, John the Baptist (Rom. 7: 4; John 3: 29).

(12.) Christ should have all pre-eminence (Col. 1: 18).

(13.) No salvation promised in any other name (Acts 4: 12).

VIII. That we should practice "closed" communion.

THE BIBLE:

1. All judgment is committed unto the Son (John 5: 22).

2. Christ commands us not to judge (Matt. 7: 1).

3. To practice either open communion (inviting all to come), or closed communion (inviting some and debarring others), is to judge a person fit or unfit and do what God will not do (He will not judge, but has committed judgment all

73

unto the Son) and do what Christ told us not to do.

4. Communion is neither open nor closed, but is just communion (I Cor. 11: 28).

5. It is the manner of partaking and not the condition of the partaker that is enjoined (I Cor. 11: 27-29).

NOTE: "Unworthily" is an adverb. It refers to the manner of partaking. If partaking depends upon a person's worthiness, then none could partake.

IX. That we do not need to commune every Lord's day.

THE BIBLE:

1. The priests partook of the shewbread in the tabernacle every week, picturing the fact that we are as members of Christ's priesthood, would partake of the communion once each week.

(1.) Things under the law a shadow of good things to come (Heb. 10: 1).

2. Early Christians communed once each week (Acts 20: 7).

3. Same phraseology as (I Cor. 16: 1, 2).

X. That we should vote members into the Church and if they sin we should vote them out of the Church.

THE BIBLE:

1. Only the Son has a right to judge (John 5: 22).

2. The Son forbids us doing any judging (Matt. 7: 1).

3. Christ says, "Let him that is without sin among you first cast a stone" (John 8: 1-11).

4. Christ says let the good and bad grow together until the end of the world (Matt. 13: 24-30, 39).
NOTE: Christ is here talking of the kingdom or the Church.

5. When a church votes a sinful member out, it is

twice as wicked as the sinner, for it breaks two commands:

(1.) Judge not that ye be not judged (Matt. 7: 1).

(2.) Let both grow together until the harvest (Matt. 13: 30).

XI. That we are baptized with the Holy Spirit.

THE BIBLE:

1. Only two cases of the baptism of the Holy Spirit in the New Testament (Acts 2: 1-4; Acts 10: 44-48).

NOTE: The first case was to endue the apostles with the Holy Spirit; the second case was to convince the Jew that the Gentile was an accepted people.

2. The baptism of the Holy Spirit gave power to perform all kinds of miracles (Acts 2: 1-2; Acts 5: 15; 20: 8-10; 28: 3-5).

NOTE: If we claim to be baptized with the Holy Spirit today, then people have the right to demand miracles of us.

XII. That we should pray for the Holy Spirit to come upon people.

THE BIBLE:

1. Christ alone has the right to pray the Holy Spirit on us (John 14: 15-17).

SEVENTH-DAY ADVENTIST

Adventism began in Massachusetts in 1831, under the leadership of Wm. Miller. In 1833, in Low Hampton, New York, he began to preach that the end of the world was at hand, publishing a pamphlet entitled, "Evidences from Scripture and History of the Second Coming of Christ about the year 1843, and of His Personal Reign of One Thousand Years".

When this prophecy failed, he declared he had erred in his calculation and set the time in 1844. This likewise failing, he set 1845 as the year. The third failure divided his followers and out of the fragments Seventh-Day Adventism was constructed. Adding some new doctrine, the principal one of which was Sabbath-keeping, that is, Saturday,—for to this time all the followers of Miller had kept Sunday—Elder James White and his wife, in 1846, became the leaders of the Seventh-Day branch of Adventism.

As a result of various divisions, there are now six bodies of Adventists, viz.: Advent Christians, Church of God, Churches of God in Jesus Christ, Evangelical Adventists, Life and Advent Union and Seventh-Day Adventists. As a rule, all these divisions now simply wait for the second coming of Christ without making any attempt to set the date thereof. Three things characterize all Adventist teaching: Prophecy, the Sabbath and the Sleep of the Soul.

Seventh-Day Adventism Teaches:

I. That there were two separate laws given at Sinai.

   1. The one written on stones which was deposited in the ark and related only to moral duties.

   2. The other given to Moses privately and written with a pen in a book which was deposited in a receptacle by the side of the ark and related only to ceremonial duties (Deut. 31: 26). (Synopsis of Present Truth, page 255.)

THE BIBLE:

I. Knows only one law (II Chron. 31: 3; Neh. 8: 2, 3, 8, 14, 18; Psa. 19: 7; Mal. 4: 4).

1. King David had a copy of the book of the law Deut. 17: 15-19).

2. The "book of the law" contained all five books of the Pentateuch.

    (1.) I Cor. 14: 34 refers to Gen. 3: 16.

    (2.) Joshua 8: 31 quotes Ex. 20: 25.

    (3.) Ezra 6: 18 quotes Num. 3: 6.

    (4.) Matt. 22: 36-40 quotes Lev. 19: 18.

    (5.) II Kings 14: 6 quotes Deut 24: 16.

3. The "Book of the Law" deposited in the receptacle by the side of the ark quotes the ten commandments twice (Ex. 20: 1-17; Deut. 5: 6-22).

4. The law of the Lord contained both so-called moral and ceremonial law (II Chron. 31: 3; Matt. 22: 36-40; Lev. 19: 1-37).

5. Moral things are holy in themselves, but ceremonial things are made holy by commandment (Mark 2: 27).

6. The Sabbath commandment is part of the ceremonial law and was made holy by commandment (Ex. 20: 8).

7. Greatest commandment not found in the decalogue (Matt. 22: 36-40; Mark 12: 29, 31).

II. That the ceremonial law "only" was nailed to the cross and that the decalogue is still binding.

THE BIBLE:

1. The law includes all of the Pentateuch.

2. The law only given to the Jew (Ex. 20: 1-17; Deut 4: 8; 5: 1; Mal. 4: 4; Rom. 2: 14).

3. The ten commandments done away (II Cor. 3: 7-11).

4. The ten commandments called a covenant (Ex.

77

34: 27, 28; Deut. 4: 12; 9: 9; I Kings 8: 9, 21;
II Chron. 5: 10; 6: 11).

5. Covenant of the decalogue abolished (Jer. 31: 31-34; Zech. 11: 10-14; Heb. 8: 6-13; Heb. 9: 15-17).

6. Decalogue consists of ordinances because they are laws, statutes and commandments and as such are done away (Eph. 2: 15; Cor. 2: 14-17).

7. The whole law done away at the cross (Acts 15: 1-11; Rom. 6: 14; 7: 1-7; Gal. 3: 23-25; 4: 1-8, 21; Heb. 7: 11-12).

8. The law was a curse and we are redeemed from the curse (Gal. 3: 13).

III. That we are to keep the Sabbath Day.

THE BIBLE:

1. The Sabbath is part of the decalogue and the ten commandments are done away (II Cor. 3: 7-11).

2. The weekly sabbath associated with meats, drinks and feast days (Num. 28: 3, 4, 9, 10, 11-15, 16; 29: 39; I Chron. 23: 30, 31; II Chron. 2: 4; 8: 13; 31: 3; Neh. 10: 33; Ezek. 45: 17).

(1.) All blotted out (Hosea 2: 11; Col. 2: 14-17).

3. Sabbath only a shadow and the shadow is supplanted by the substance (Heb. 4: 1-11; 10: 1; Gal. 4: 10, 11).

4. Apostles never taught Sabbath keeping, but they DID teach meeting upon the first day of the week (Acts 20: 7; I Cor. 16: 1-2).

NOTE: If it was intended that we should keep the Sabbath it is strange that the apostles did not teach the heathen, who knew nothing about Sabbath keeping, to keep the Sabbath.

5. All days are of equal importance now (Rom. 14: 5).

IV. That the decalogue was not done away in the abolition of the old covenant.

"If the ten commandments constituted the old covenant, then they are gone forever." (Two Covenants, page 5, Elder Smith.)

THE BIBLE:

1. The ten commandments are called a covenant (Ex. 34: 27, 28; Deut. 4: 12, 13; Deut. 5: 2-7; 9: 9; I Kings 8: 9, 21; II Chron. 5: 10; 6: 11).

    (1.) A covenant is an agreement between two people to do a certain thing.

        (Ex. 19: 3-8) People promise to obey.

        (Ex. 19: 9-25) People prepare to hear God's voice.

        (Ex. 20: 1-17) God speaks the ten commandments to the people.

        (Ex. 24: 3) Moses rehearses to the people the words of the Lord.

        (Ex. 24: 3) The people agree to obey.

        (Ex. 24: 4) Moses wrote all the words of the Lord in a book and read it to them.

        (Ex. 24: 7) The third time the people agreed to obey.

        (Ex. 24: 8) Moses sealed this covenant with blood.

    (2.) This is the first covenant because Paul, quoting (Ex. 24: 8), calls it the first covenant (Heb. 9: 18-20).

        a. The decalogue was written on stones called the "tables of the covenant" (Ex. 24: 7).

        b. The decalogue was written in a book called the "book of the covenant" (Ex. 24: 7).

        c. The ark in which the decalogue was placed is called the ark of the covenant (Deut. 31: 26).

2. It was prophesied that the covenant was to be

done away (Jer. 31: 31-34). Israel broke this covenant.

3. The prophecy fulfilled (Heb. 8: 6-13). Paul quotes (Jer. 31: 31-34), and says it is fulfilled in the Gospel.

4. The decalogue covenant is done away (II Cor. 3: 3-11; Gal. 4: 21-24).

5. Christians do not go to Mt. Sinai or the Old Testament or covenant any more, but to Jesus and the new covenant (Heb. 12: 18-24).

6. The ark of the covenant is to be forgotten (Jer. 3: 16, 17).

7. The new covenant is sealed with blood (Heb. 9: 11-22; Col. 2: 14).

V. That the soul sleeps after death.

1. God is the Father of spirits (John 3: 6; Acts 17: 29; James 2: 26).

2. Paul speaks of the spirits of just men made perfect (Heb. 12: 22-24).

3. The spirit does not die with the body (Eccl. 3: 21; 12: 7; Luke 23: 42, 43; Acts 7: 59; II Cor. 4: 16; 5: 1-8).

4. The departed spirits are conscious (Matt. 17: 3; 22: 32; Luke 16: 19-31; Rev. 6: 9-11; I Peter 3: 18-21).

5. The body is said to sleep in the grave, but not the spirit (Matt. 27: 52).

VI. That it doesn't make any difference what name you wear.

1. Adam and his wife wore the same name (Gen. 5: 2).

2. Adam is a type of Christ (Rom. 5: 14).

NOTE: Adam being a type or figure of Christ, then his wife would be a type of Christ's wife —the Church. Adam and his wife wearing the same name and both being types pictures the fact that Christ and His wife should wear the same name.

3. It was prophesied that when salvation went out from Jerusalem and the Gentiles should see righteousness that a new name should be given by the mouth of the Lord.

4. This prophecy fulfilled.

    (1.) Salvation went out from Jerusalem (Luke 24: 47; Acts 2: 1-47).

    (2.) The Gentiles saw His righteousness (Acts 10: 1-48; 11: 1).

    (3.) The new name was immediately given when these prophecies were fulfilled (Acts 11: 25, 26).

NOTE: The name, "Christian", is a new name. The name, disciple, is not new, for Moses had disciples. The name, "brethren", is not a new name, for they were called brethren in the Old Testament. The name, "saint", is not a new name, for they were called saints in times past, but the name, "Christian", is absolutely new.

5. We are to suffer in the name, "Christian" (I Peter 4: 16).

6. There is no salvation promised in any other name (Acts 4: 12).

VII. That the observance of the Lord's Supper at regular intervals is unimportant.

THE BIBLE:

1. The early Church observed the Lord's Supper weekly (Acts 2: 42; Acts 20: 7).

2. There is no life in us if we do not observe this (John 6: 53).

VIII. That we may expect Christ's return any time now.

NOTE: The Adventists had set dates for the second advent of Christ in 1843, Oct. 1844. (Life Incidents, pp. 72, 166, 167), 1845. (A Word for the Little Flock, by James White,

p. 22), 1847, '50, '52, '54, '55, '63, '66, '68, '77 (dates set by other Adventists).

THE BIBLE:

1. There is to come a time of blessedness when man's length of life shall be increased, when man shall enjoy the labor of his hands, when the land shall bring forth abundantly, when prayer shall be answered before the call is made, and when peace shall reign supreme, and since this has not come yet, Christ can not return (Isa. 65: 20-25).

2. The heavens must receive Christ until the restitution of all things (Acts 3: 20, 21).
   NOTE: There are still thorns whereas before the curse was placed on the earth there were none.

3. The Jews are yet to believe before Christ returns (Rom. 11: 1-36).

4. He is to come when all enemies have been put under His feet and when the last enemy, which is death, shall be destroyed (I Cor. 15: 24-26).
   NOTE: There still is death.

WHAT THE LAW COULD NOT DO

1. No man is justified by the law (Gal. 2: 16).

2. Those looking to the law for salvation are called fools by Paul (Gal. 2: 16).

3. No Old Testament law was based on faith, therefore could not save, for "the just shall live by faith" (Gal. 3: 11, 12; Rom. 1: 17; Heb. 11: 6).

4. All under the law were under the curse (Gal. 3: 13).

5. No inheritance through any Old Testament law (Gal. 3: 18).

6. The law was not given to save people, but to bring a Saviour (Gal. 3: 19).

7. If any Old Testament law could have given life, Christ would not have come (Gal. 3: 21).

8. Those under the law had to be redeemed (Gal. 4: 1-5).
9. Those who keep the law are fallen from grace (Gal. 5: 4).

All quotations taken from Synopsis of Present Truth and Two Covenants.

MORMONISM

The Mormon Church was organized April 6, 1830. at Fayette, N. Y., with six members, by Joseph Smith, known as "Peep-Stone Joe", because following in the steps of his father as a roving water witch, he claimed to have miraculously discovered a "peep-stone". At the age of fourteen Smith began to have visions and revelations. According to his alleged statement three years later he had a vision one night in which the angel Moroni appeared unto him and revealed the hiding place of certain plates of gold on which was inscribed the Gospel. With the aid of Harris, Cowdery and Whitmer, Smith is supposed to have translated this writing into what is now called the Book of Mormon. In 1831 Smith and a small company of converts moved to Kirtland, Ohio, but because of a scandal which occurred there they moved to Missouri. Trouble breaking out here, Smith and about fifteen thousand followers went to Nauvoo, Ill. It was here that the doctrine of polygamy was introduced, although Mormons had been accused before this of unholy relationship with numerous women.

Internal trouble arose at Nauvoo and public opinion ran high against the Mormons. Finally Smith and his brother, Hyrum were arrested on a charge of treason and lodged in the jail at Carthage. Here a mob broke into the jail and shot the two brothers. After Smith's death the Mormons split into several divisions, one under the leadership of J. J. Strang, went to Wisconsin, but died out upon the death of its leader: another group formed the Reorganized Church of Jesus Christ of Latter Day Saints, but the main body, under the leadership of Brigham Young, immigrated in 1848 to Utah. This, even today, is by far the largest body of Mormons and has its headquarters in Salt Lake City.

GOD

Mormonism Teaches:

I That there are many gods.

"A general assembly, quorum or grand council

of the gods, with their president at their head, constitute the designing and creating power" (Key of Theology, page 52.)

THE BIBLE:

1. There is only one God with three in the Godhead (Gen. 1: 26; Ex. 20: 1-3; Matt. 28: 19; John 1: 1-3; John 14: 25, 26; John 16: 7-10).

II. That these Gods have bodies of bones and flesh. "That which is without body, parts and passions is nothing. There is no other God in heaven, but that God who has flesh and bones. The Father has a body of flesh and bones as tangible as man's." (D. and C., Sec. 130: 22.)

THE BIBLE:

1. God is an omnipresent Being (Psa. 139: 7-11; Acts 17: 28; I Cor. 3: 16).

2. God is an omniscient Being (Job 34: 21; Prov. 15: 3; John 2: 24, 24).

3. God is an omnipotent Being (Gen. 1: 1; Psa. 8: 3; 19: 1; John 1: 1-3).
   NOTE: If God has flesh and bones as a man, He could not be any of these three.

4. God is a Spirit (John 4: 24; Luke 24: 39; I Cor. 15: 50).

III. That the gods have sex and marry and bear children and their children come to this world as human beings to get bodies. (Compendium (B) 287, Last sermon 1844.)

"God, angels and men are all of one species, one race, one great family" (Key of Theology, page 41.)

"Wisdom inspires the gods to multiply their species." (Key of Theology, page 52.)

"Each god, through his wife or wives, raises up a numerous family of sons and daughters" (The Seer, Vol. 1, page 37.)

85

THE BIBLE:

1. God's only marriage relationship is with Israel (Jer. 3: 14).

2. Christ's only marriage relationship is with Christians (Eph. 5: 23-33).

3. Christ is the husband and head of the Church (John 3: 29; Col. 1: 18).

4. No marriage relationship after death (Mark 12: 25).

IV.   That Adam is God and the father of our race.
"Now hear it, O inhabitants of the earth, Jew and Gentile, saint and sinner. When our father Adam came into the Garden of Eden, he came into it with a celestial body and brought Eve, one of his wives, with him. He helped to make and organize the world. He is Michael, the archangel, the Ancient of Days, about whom holy men have written and spoken. He is our Father and our God, and the only God with whom we have to do." (Journal of Discourses, Vol. 6, page 50.) (Pearl of Great Price, page 60.)

THE BIBLE:

1. Adam is not God, but was created by God (Gen. 1: 27; 2: 18, 20-25; 3: 8-11, 19; Ex. 20: 1-3).

V.   That God is an exalted man who was once as we are and that we are to become like Him.
"God himself was once as we are now and is an exalted man and sits enthroned in yonder heavens." (Journal of Discourses, Vol. 6, page 3, sermon by Joseph Smith.)
"And you have got to learn how to be gods yourselves . . . . the same as all gods have done before you." (Journal of Discourses, Vol. 6, page 5, sermon by Joseph Smith.)

THE BIBLE:

1. Man is a created being (Gen. 2: 7).

2. Christ from His fleshly side only was like us (Isa. 7: 14; Matt. 1: 20-23).
3. No man hath ascended into heaven but Christ, proving that Adam or none before Christ ever went to heaven and that none could have become gods (John 3: 13).

CHRIST

Mormonism Teaches:

I. That Adam is God and that Christ is his son by natural generation.

"He (Adam) is our father and our God . . . . when the Virgin Mary conceived the child Jesus, the Father had begotten Him in His own likeness. He was not begotten by the Holy Spirit. And who is the Father? He is the first of the human family." (Journal of Discourses, Vol. 1, page 50, sermon by Brigham Young.)

The Bible:

1. Christ was born of the Holy Spirit (Isa. 7: 14; Matt. 1: 18-23).

II. That Jesus was a polygamist.

"If none but God's will be permitted to multiply immortal children, it follows that each god must have one or more wives. The evangelists do not particularly speak of the marriage of Jesus, but one thing is certain, that there were several holy women that greatly loved Jesus, such as Mary and Martha, her sister, and Mary Magdalene; and Jesus greatly loved them, and associated with them much . . . . if all the acts of Jesus were written, we, no doubt, should learn that these beloved women were His wives." (The Seer, Vol. 1, page 158, 159.)

Note: If Christ is the Son of a fleshly God, then He is the son of the god of this world—the devil. This would make Christ a sinner (John 8: 44).

THE BIBLE:

1. Christ is the husband of the Church (John 3: 29; Rom. 7: 4; Eph. 5: 23-33).

THE HOLY SPIRIT

MORMONISM TEACHES:

I. That the Holy Spirit is ethereal substance diffused through space, the purest and most refined of substances.

THE BIBLE:

1. The Holy Spirit is a personality (Matt. 28: 19; John 14: 15-17; John 16: 13, 14; Acts 5: 3, 4; 8: 29; 10: 19, 20; I John 5: 7).

II. That there is only one mode by which the Holy Spirit is conferred and that is by the laying on of hands.

THE BIBLE:

The Holy Spirit is given in three degrees.

1. Baptismal (Acts 2: 1-4; 10: 44-47; 11: 15).

2. By the laying on of an apostle's hands (Acts 8: 12-17; 19: 6; I Tim. 4: 14; II Tim. 1: 6).
   NOTE: None but an apostle could confer the Holy Spirit by the laying on of hands and the apostles have no successors, for since an apostle means witness and a witness can have no successor, then the apostles could have no successors.
   Spiritual gifts are conferred by the laying on of hands of an apostle and where no apostle had gone the Church was without spiritual gifts (Rom. 1: 9-11).

3. The general gift of the Holy Spirit after baptism as a Comforter or counselor (Acts 2: 39; John 14: 15-17).

III. That the Holy Spirit can be conferred today by the laying on of hands.

The Bible:

1. Only the apostles were witnesses of Christ and they only could confer the Holy Spirit by the laying on of hands (Acts 8: 12-17; Acts 19: 6; I Tim. 4: 14; II Tim. 1: 6).

2. The apostles are dead and have no successors.

THE BIBLE

Mormonism Teaches:

I. That the Bible is not all of the Word of God.

"Thou fool, that shall say, A Bible, a Bible, we have got a Bible, and we need no other Bible . . . . ye need not suppose that it contains all my words; neither need ye suppose that I have not caused more to be written." (Book of Mormon, II Nephi 12: 53-64.)

"And they shall remain under the condemnation until they repent and remember the new covenant, even the Book of Mormon and the former commandments which I have given them." (D. and C., Sec. 84: 57).

"And if thou shalt receive revelation upon revelation" (D. and C. 42: 17).

II. That the Book of Mormon and the Doctrine and Covenants are on a par with the Bible.

"Has God given many revelations to men? Ans. Yes; a great number. Where have we any account of his doing so? Ans. In the Bible, the Book of Mormons, the Book of Doctrine and Covenants, and other publications of the Church of Jesus Christ of Latter-day Saints." (Catechism, Chap. III, Questions 1 and 2.)

III. That the Bible has scarcely a verse that is not polluted.

"Indeed, no one, without further revelation, knows whether even one-hundredth part of the doctrines and ordinances of salvation are contained in the few books of Scripture which have descended to our times; how, then, can it be decided that they are a sufficient guide ?

What shall we say, then, concerning the Bible being a sufficient guide? Can we rely upon it in its present known corrupted state as being a faithful record of God's word? We all know that but a few of the inspired writings have descended to our times, which few quote the names of some twenty other books which are lost, and it is quite certain that there were many other inspired books that even the names have not reached us. What few have come down to our day have been mutilated, changed and corrupted in such a shameful manner that no two manuscripts agree.

Verses and even whole chapters have been added by unknown persons and even we do not know the authors of some whole books. Who knows that even one verse of the whole Bible has escaped pollution, so as to convey the same sense now that it did in the original? (Divine Authenticity of the Book of Mormon, pages 204, 205, 218 Orson Pratt.)

The Bible:

(Isa. 8: 20; Rev. 22: 18, 19).

Note: There are probably not less than ten thousand verses of the Bible to be found in the Book of Mormon, yet Mr. Pratt says it is doubtful that even one verse of the Bible has escaped pollution. If this be true, where does the Book of Mormon appear?

SALVATION

Mormonism Teaches:

1. That salvation is the resurrection of the dead.
   "And the resurrection of the dead is the redemption of the soul" (D. and C. 88: 16).

THE BIBLE:

1. Both good and bad are to be resurrected (Rev. 20: 11-15).

   NOTE: If resurrection means salvation, and both good and bad are resurrected, then that would be universal salvation.

II. That salvation consists of three degrees.

   "The highest" or "celestial", those who have believed, have been baptized by a Mormon, have had hands laid on by a Mormon elder for the 'conveying of the Holy Ghost,' who are thus the 'church of the first-born,' who will be taken up when Christ comes in the clouds, raised in the first resurrection to dwell with God and Christ forever and reign over the earth with bodies celestial.

   "The second, or 'terrestial'; those who died without law (Heathen); the spirits in prison, to whom Christ went and preached and who received His message; those who were blinded by craftiness of men; those will have the presence of Christ, but not that of the Father, with 'terrestrial bodies'.

   "The third, or those who did not receive the Gospel, did not deny the Spirit are thrust down to hell till the last resurrection; who say they are of Paul and Apollos and Cephas, Christ, etc., but did not accept Mormonism; who are liars, sorcerers, and other vile things; at the last resurrection shall be judged and shall receive mansions according to their works, but where God and Christ dwell they can not come, worlds without end" (Doc. and Cov. 76: 51-112).

THE BIBLE:

(Matt. 20: 1-16; Matt. 25: 14-30; Matt. 28: 19; John 14: 11: I John 3: 2; Rev. 22: 4.)

III. That the dead may be saved by a living person being baptized for them.

"That they, my saints, may be baptized for those who are dead; for this ordinance belongeth to my house . . . . for which the same was instituted from the foundation of the world" (Doc. and Cov. 124: 28).

"God has made a provision that every spirit in the eternal world can be ferreted out and saved, unless he has committed that unpardonable sin (disobeying the Gospel). And so you can see how far you can be a saviour." (Journal of Discourses, Vol. 6, pages 7, 8, Joseph Smith, speaking.)

THE BIBLE:

1. Command to obey baptism is based on hearing, believing and repenting (Rom. 10: 13-17; Matt. 28: 19, 20; Mark 16: 15, 16; Luke 13: 3; Acts 2: 38; Rev. 20: 12, 13).

THE CHURCH

MORMONISM TEACHES:

I. That there can be no true church today without living apostles and prophets.

THE BIBLE:

1. The Church was not founded upon the personalities of the apostles and prophets, but upon the Divine teachings which they revealed (II Peter 1: 21; Acts 1: 1-3; II Peter 3: 1-3).
NOTE: If we are to have living apostles and prophets today to have a New Testament Church, then we must have a personal, living Christ on earth (Eph. 2: 20).

2. An apostle is a witness (Luke 1: 2; 24: 33; Acts 1: 1-3, 19-22; 10: 39-41; I Cor. 9: 1; I Cor. 15: 5, 7, 8; II Peter 1: 16; I John 1: 1). A witness can have no successor, so there can be no apostles personally in the Church today.

3. The twelve were to sit on twelve thrones (Matt. 19: 28, 29). Every Mormon apostle will have to stand up since there is no seat left for him.

4. Miracles are a sign of apostleship (II Cor. 12: 12).

5. So-called Mormon apostles are false apostles, for they usurp the signs of an apostle (II Cor. 11: 13).

PROPHETS

Mormonism Teaches:

1. That Joseph Smith was a prophet and makes belief in him as such, an essential article of faith.

   "But, behold, verily, verily, I say unto thee, no one shall be appointed to receive commandments and revelations in this church excepting my servant Joseph Smith, Jr., for he receiveth them, even as Moses" (Doc. and Cov., Sec. 28: 2).

   "And I have sent forth the fullness of my gospel by the hand of my servant Joseph" (Doc. and Cov., Sec. 35: 17).

   "Every spirit that confesses that Joseph Smith is a prophet, that he lived and died a prophet, and that the Book of Mormon is true, is of God, and every spirit that does not is of "Anti-Christ." (Millennial Star, Vol. 5, page 118, Brigham Young.)

The Bible:

1. True prophecy has been given (I Cor. 13: 8; Gal. 1: 7-9; Rev. 22: 18, 19).

2. Many false prophets were to come (Matt. 7: 15; 24: 11; II Cor. 11: 13; II Peter 2: 1; I John 4: 1).

   NOTE: This makes provision for Joseph Smith.

98

MARMIAGE

MORMONISM TEACHES:

I. That there are two kinds of marriages, earthly and
celestial.

   1. The earthly marriage bond is to have as many
child-bearing wives as possible to insure a great
kingdom in heaven. It is for life and eternity.
"Each God, through his wife or wives, raises up
a numerous family of sons and daughters . . . .
for each father and mother will be in a condition to multiply forever and ever." (The Seer,
Vol. 1, page 37.)

   2. The celestial marriage bond is a sealing of other
men's wives to a man so that he may have
enough wives in eternity. Women only who
have proved their capacity in child-bearing here
are desirable for celestial wives. That means
men covet other men's wives. This is for eternity only.

THE BIBLE:

1. Child-bearing was to replenish the earth, not
heaven (Gen. 1: 28).

2. They neither marry nor are given in marriage in
heaven (Mark 12: 25; Luke 12: 35; Ex. 20:
17).

3. NOTE: How is the marriage relationship to be
maintained in eternity when one is a vile sinner
and the other a saint?

3. The woman is freed from her dead husband (I
Cor. 7: 39).

POLYGAMY

MORMONISM TEACHES:

I. That polygamy is a law to be obeyed and if dis-
obeyed damnation is the penalty.

"If none but God's will be permitted to multiply immortal children, it follows that each God
must have one or more wives." (The Seer, Vol.
1, page 158.)

"All those who have this law (plural or celestial marriage) revealed unto them must obey the same . . . . and if ye abide not in that covenant, then are ye damned; for no one can reject this covenant and be permitted to enter into my glory . . . . as pertaining to the new and everlasting covenant, it was instituted for the fullness of my glory; and he that receiveth a fullness thereof must and shall abide in the law, or he shall be damned, saith the Lord God" (D. and C., Sec. 132: 3, 4, 6).

"And again, as pertaining to the law of the priesthood; if any man . . . . have ten virgins given unto him by this law, he can not commit adultery, for they belong to him" (D. and C., Sec. 132: 61, 62).

THE BIBLE:

1. Man is to cleave to his "wife", not wives (Gen. 1: 18-25).
2. As Christ has one Church, man has one wife (Eph. 5: 23-33).
3. Church officers to be the husband of one wife (I Tim. 3: 2).
4. A murderer, Lamech, originated polygamy (Gen. 4: 19-24).

COMMUNION

MORMONISM:

I. Uses water in the place of fruit of the vine in the Lord's Supper.

THE BIBLE:

1. Fruit of the vine is always used (Matt. 26: 26-29; Mark 14: 22-25; I Cor. 11: 20-34).

NAME

MORMONISM TEACHES:

I. That it is Scriptural to wear other names, wearing the names of Latter-day Saints and Mormon.

THE BIBLE:

1. Adam and his wife wore the same name (Gen. 5: 2).
2. Adam is a figure of Christ (Rom. 5: 14).
3. Adam and his wife wearing the same name is a picture of Christ and his wife—the Church—wearing the same name.
4. Prophesied God's people would be given a NEW name (Isa. 62: 1, 2).
5. Prophecy fulfilled (Acts 2: 1-47; Acts 10: 1-48; Acts 11: 1).

   NOTE: Prophecy fulfilled in that salvation had gone out from Jerusalem and the Gentiles had seen His righteousness.

6. The new name given—Christian (Acts 11: 25, 26).
7. Agrippa knew the followers of Christ wore that name (Acts 26: 28).
8. We are married to Christ and this shows marriage relationship (John 3: 29; Rom. 7: 4).
9. We are to suffer in the name, Christian, (I Peter 4: 16).
10. We are to wear Christ's name in two worlds (Rev. 22: 4).
11. No salvation promised in any other name (Acts 4: 12).

All quotations taken from the following books:

> Key of Theology
> Doctrine and Covenants
> Journal of Discourses
> The Seer
> Book of Mormon

RUSSELLISM

Russellism is a mixture of Universalism, Unitarianism, Adventism and Materialism. This conglomeration of religious vagaries was originated by Charles T. Russell, commonly called "Pastor Russell". He first published his tenets under the name of "Millennial Dawn", but later brought them out under the title of "Studies in the Scriptures". His writings were mostly un-Scriptural and anti-Scriptural, although there was just enough truth in them to make them plausible enough to be doubly deceiving. He enriched himself greatly from the sale of his books.

Mr. Russell's character as a man was nothing of which to boast. The courts of Pennsylvania ruled that he tried to perpetuate a fraud upon his wife and denied his plea of being penniless when his wife sued him for divorce. It later developed that he had transferred $317,000 to the Watch-tower Bible and Tract Society, of which he was president, seemingly with the intent to avoid paying his wife alimony. His wife obtained her divorce from him on account of his unmanly conduct and gross familiarity with other women. Open court testimony concerning his character recorded him saying of himself, "I am like a jelly-fish; I float around here and there; I touch this one and that one, and if she responds, I take her to me, and if not, I float to others."

Pastor Russell taught that Jesus Christ and his apostles came to earth in October, 1874, and have been here ever since. He further predicted that the consummation of the ages would occur in 1914.

Russellism Teaches:

I. That one can not have the true light without the help of "Studies in the Scriptures", first called "Millennial Dawn".

"If any one lays 'Scriptural Studies' aside even after he has become familiar with them, even

97

after he has read them ten years, and goes to the Bible alone, though he has understood his Bible for ten years, our experience shows that within two years he goes into darkness." (Watch-Tower, Sept. 15, 1910, page 298.)

"If the six volumes of Scripture Studies are practically the Bible topically arranged, with Bible-proofs given, we might not improperly name the volumes—The Bible in arranged form. That is to say, they are not merely comments on the Bible, but they are practically the Bible itself." (Same page above.)

THE BIBLE:

1. God's Word is the lamp and light (Psa. 119: 105).

2. The Bible is sufficient to perfect the man of God (II Tim. 3: 16, 17).

GOD

RUSSELLISM TEACHES:

I. There is only one person in the God-head.

"The careful student of the preceding chapters has found abundant testimony from the Scriptures, to the effect that there is but one Almighty God." (Vol. 5, page 166.)

"Verily, if it were not for the fact that this Trinitarian nonsense was drilled into us from earliest infancy, and the fact that it is soberly taught in Theological Seminaries by gray-haired professors, in many other ways apparently wise, nobody would give it a moment's consideration." (Vol. 5: page 166.)

THE BIBLE:

1. Baptism is into the name of three personalities (Matt. 28: 19).

2. Christ taught three personalities in the God-head (John 14: 15, 16, 26; 15: 26).

CHRIST

I. That Christ was a "created angel" before He came to this earth.

"As He (Christ) is the highest of Jehovah's creation, so also He was the first, the direct creation of God, the only begotten." (Vol. 5, page 84.)

The Bible:

1. Christ was more than an angel (Heb. 1: 1-8).
2. Christ was not created—He was eternal (John 1: 1-3; 8: 58; Rev. 1: 8; 21: 6; 22: 13).

II. That Christ was not a combination of two natures —human and divine.

"Neither was Jesus a combination of the two natures, human and spiritual . . . . When Jesus was in the flesh He was a perfect human being and since His resurrection He is a perfect spiritual being of the highest or divine order." (Vol. 1, page 179.)

The Bible:

1. Prophesied that God would tabernacle in the flesh (Isa. 7: 14; Matt. 1: 23).
2. Christ was begotten of the Holy Spirit and born of Mary, making two natures, human and divine (Matt. 1: 18-20).
3. Christ was made in the likeness of man (Phil. 2: 6, 7; Heb. 2: 16).
4. Christ was human and divine (John 1: 1, 2, 14; 16: 28; I Tim. 3: 16).
5. Peter confessed Him as the Son of God (Matt. 16: 16).
6. He who does not confess that Christ came in the flesh is a deceiver and not of God (I John 4: 3; II John 7).

III. That Christ did not atone for the sins of the race. "We shall see subsequently, when we come to consider particularly the ransom feature of His work, that it was absolutely necessary that He should be a man—neither more nor less than a perfect man." (Vol. 5: 95.)

THE BIBLE:

1. Christ taketh away sins (John 1: 29; Matt. 10: 28; Rom. 5: 11; Heb. 10: 3-14).

IV. That Christ's body was not raised from the dead. "Our Lord's human body was, however, supernaturally removed from the tomb; because, had it remained there, it would have been an insurmountable obstacle to the faith of the disciples. We know nothing about what became of it, except that it did not decay or corrupt. Whether it was dissolved into gasses, or whether it is still preserved somewhere as the grand memorial of God's love, of Christ's obedience, and of our redemption, no one knows; nor is such knowledge necessary." (Vol. 2, pages 125-130.)

THE BIBLE:

1. Jesus said He would raise His body (John 2: 19-22).

2. Jesus showed Thomas His raised body (John 20: 24-28).

V. That Christ is forever dead. "It was necessary, not only that the man Christ Jesus should die, but just as necessary that the man Christ Jesus should never live again, should remain dead, should remain our ransom-price for all eternity." (Vol. 5, page 443.)

THE BIBLE:

1. Prophesied that Christ would be resurrected (Psa. 16: 10).

2. Peter said Christ was raised from the dead (Acts 2: 30, 31).

3. Christ showed Himself alive by many infallible proofs (Acts 1: 1-3).

4. Christ was seen alive by many brethren (1 Cor. 15: 1-8).

VI. That Jesus was not divine until after His resurrection.

"The human nature had to be consecrated to death before He could receive even the pledge of the divine nature. And not until that consecration was actually carried out and He had actually sacrificed the human nature, even unto death, did our Lord Jesus become a full partaker of the divine nature." (Vol. 1, page 179.)

THE BIBLE:

1. Christ was always divine (John 1: 1-3; 17: 5).
2. Christ was equal with God (Phil. 2: 6).
3. Christ and God are one (John 14: 11; 17: 21).

VII. That Christ was no longer the same person after the resurrection.

"If our Lord is still" the man Christ Jesus . . . then instead of being exalted higher than angels, and every name that is named in heaven as well as in earth, He is still a man."

THE BIBLE:

1. The Bible says He is the same person after resurrection (Acts 1: 11; Eph. 4: 10; Heb. 10: 12).

VIII. That Christ is not a Mediator.

"In our issue of 1906, page 26, we said, 'Our Lord Jesus, in His own person, has been the Mediator, between the Father and the household of faith, during the Gospel age.' This statement is incorrect. No Scripture so declares. It is a part of the smoke of the dark ages, which we are glad to now wipe from our

101

eyes." (Watch Tower, Sept. 15, 1909, page 283.)

THE BIBLE:

1. Christ is our Mediator (I Tim. 2: 5; Heb. 9: 15; I John 2: 1).

THE HOLY SPIRIT

RUSSELLISM TEACHES:

I. That the Holy Spirit is only the influence or power exercised by the one God.

"And equally consistent is the Scripture teaching respecting the Holy Spirit—that it is not another God, but the spirit, influence or power exercised by the one God, our Father." (Vol. 5, page 165.)

THE BIBLE:

1. The Holy Spirit is part of the God-head (Matt. 3: 16, 17; Matt. 28: 19).

2. The Holy Spirit is called God (Acts 5: 3, 4).

II. That the Holy Spirit is not a personality. (See above statement.)

THE BIBLE:

1. "He" can teach (John 14: 26).

2. "He" can talk (Acts 8: 29; 10: 19, 20).

3. "He" can testify (John 15: 26).

4. "He" selects fields of labor and sends preachers (Acts 13: 2; 16: 6-10).

5. These are attributes of personality.

THE KINGDOM

1. That the kingdom is not yet established.

"To whom it is the Father's good pleasure to give the kingdom in an age to follow this" (the Gospel-age.) (Vol. 1, page 172.)

II. That the kingdom is not to be established until the Millennium.

"In the end of this age, and the dawn of its successor, the Millennial age, Satan is to be bound and his power overthrown, preparatory to the establishment of Christ's kingdom." Vol. i, page 73.)

THE BIBLE:

1. John and Jesus preached the kingdom at hand in their day (Matt. 3: 2; 4: 17).
2. Jesus said some in His generation would not taste death until the kingdom should come (Matt. 16: 28; Mark 9: 1).
3. We today are translated into the kingdom of God's dear Son (Col. 1: 13).
   NOTE: How could we be translated into a kingdom if it did not already exist?

SIN

RUSSELLISM TEACHES:

I. That each does not die for his own sin, but for Adam's sin.

"The day in which every man (who dies) shall die for his own sin, only, is the Millennial or restitution day." (Vol. 1, page 109.)

THE BIBLE:

1. We do not die for Adam's sin, but our own (Rom. 5: 12).
2. All have sinned and come short of the glory (Rom. 3: 23).

CONVERSION

RUSSELLISM TEACHES:

I. That God is not trying to convert sinners in the Gospel-age, but that conversion begins in the Millennium.

"The conversion of the world in the present age was not expected of the Church, but her mission has been to preach the Gospel in all the world for a witness, and to prepare herself under

divine direction for her great future work."
(Vol. I, page 95.)

"When the called out company (called to be sons of God, heirs of God, and joint-heirs with Jesus Christ our Lord—who have made their calling and election sure) is complete, then the plan of God for the world's salvation will be only beginning." (Vol. 1, page 98.)

THE BIBLE:

1. Christ commanded the Gospel to be preached to save sinners (Mark 16: 15, 16).

2. Salvation is offered before the Millennium (Acts 2: 40; 13: 26, 47).

3. Paul says today is the day of salvation (II Cor. 6: 2; Phil. 2: 12).

4. Paul says God now commandeth all men everywhere to repent (Acts 17: 30).

5. Paul says we can not escape if we neglect so great salvation (Heb. 2: 3, 4).

SALVATION

RUSSELLISM TEACHES:

I. That salvation is by faith only.

"The only ground of salvation mentioned in the Scriptures is faith in Christ as our Redeemer and Lord. 'By grace are ye saved through faith.'" (Vol. 1, page 100.)

THE BIBLE:

1. Faith without works is dead (James 2: 17).

2. Abraham's faith was justified by works (James 2: 21).

3. James says we are not justified by faith only (James 2: 24).

4. Faith without works is dead (James 2: 26).

5. If faith alone would save, then every devil would be saved. That would be universal salvation (James 2: 19).

A SECOND CHANCE

I. That every man shall have another chance.

"The 'ransom for all' given by 'th e man Christ Jesus' does not give nor guarantee everlasting life or blessing to any man; but it does guarantee to every man another opportunity or trial for life everlasting." Vol. 1, page 150.)

"The second chance will be more favorable than the first because of the experience gained under the results of the first trial." (Vol. 1, page 143.)

"All were sentenced to death because of Adam's disobedience, and all will enjoy (in this life or in the next) a full opportunity to gain everlasting life under the favorable terms of the New Covenant." (Vol. I, pages 130, 131.)

THE BIBLE:

1. No second chance taught in the Bible (Luke 9: 59-62; 16: 19-31; Acts 13: 44-46; 18: 5, 6; II Thes. 2: 10-12; Heb. 10: 26).

2. Given to men to die and then the judgment (Heb. 9: 27)

DEATH

RUSSELLISM TEACHES:

I. That death is a destruction.

"The penalty is death, not dying; and death is the absence of life, destruction." (Vol. 5: 465.)

II. That death is annihilation.

"It should be remembered, however, that it is not the pain and suffering in dying, but death— the extinction of life—in which the dying culminates, that is the penalty of sin." (Vol. 1, page 154.)

III. That death is unconsciousness.

"As the natural sleep, if sound, implies total unconsciousness, so with death, the figurative sleep; it is a period of absolute unconsciousness; more than that, it is a period of absolute non-existence." (Vol. 5, page 329.)

THE BIBLE:

1. Jesus said that killing the body does not kill the soul (Matt. 10: 28).

2. Jesus said that Abraham, Isaac and Jacob still lived, even though their bodies were dead (Matt. 22: 32).

3. Moses and Elijah still lived though their bodies were dead (Matt. 17: 3).

4. Death does not mean extinction, for the spirits of men live after their bodies are dead (Heb. 12: 22, 23).

5. The soul is conscious after death (Rev. 6: 9 11).

HELL

RUSSELLISM TEACHES:

I. That there is no eternal punishment.

"The theory of eternal punishment is inconsistent with the statements that 'the Lord hath laid upon him the iniquity of us all,' and that Christ 'died for our sins.' " (Vol. 1, page 159.)

"It is absurd to suppose that God would perpetuate Adam's existence forever in torment for any kind of a sin which he could commit, but especially for the comparatively small offense of eating forbidden fruit." (Vol. 1, page 159.)

THE BIBLE:

1. There is an eternal punishment (Dan. 12: 2; Matt. 25: 46; John 5: 28, 29; Rev. 20: 10).
NOTE: The same Greek word is used in Matt. 25: 46 to qualify punishment and life.

THE LORD'S SUPPER

RUSSELLISM TEACHES:

I. That the Lord's Supper took the place of the Passover feast.

"Our Lord's evident intention was to fix in the minds of his followers the fact that he is the antitypical Lamb to the antitypical first-borns and household of faith. 'This do in remembrance of me' implies that this new institution should take the place with his followers of the former one.'" (The Passover.) (Vol. 6, page 462.)

THE BIBLE:

1. The Passover feast was observed in memory of their passing out of Egypt (Deut. 16).

2. The Lord's Supper could not take the place of this Passover, because it was observed for another purpose—to remember Christ's death (Luke 22: 19).

II. That the Lord's Supper should be observed annually. "We would not understand this to imply the doing of it without respect of time and place, etc., but as signifying that when this cup and unleavened bread thenceforth were used as a celebration of the Passover . . . . as it would not have been lawful, proper or typical to celebrate the Passover at any other time than that appointed of the Lord, likewise it is still not appropriate to celebrate the antitype at any other time than its anniversary." (Vol. 6, page 462-9.)

THE BIBLE:

2. Early church observed the Lord's Supper every week (Acts 20: 7).

2. NOTE: The same phraseology is found in (I Cor. 16: 1, 2) and all understand that in the latter reference weekly collection is taught. Also the same phraseology is found in the command, "Remember the Sabbath to keep it holy." Every Jew understood this to be a command to keep every Sabbath.

BAPTISM

RUSSELLISM TEACHES:

I. That baptism is added to the scheme of redemption.

II. That water baptism symbolizes the baptism of the heart.

THE BIBLE:

1. Baptism is part of the plan of redemption (Mark 16: 15, 16; (John 3: 5; Acts 2: 38; Acts 8: 26-39; 22: 16; Gal. 3: 27; I Peter 3: 21).

2. Baptism symbolizes the death, burial and resurrection of Christ (Rom. 6: 4, 5).

TIME SETTING

RUSSELLISM TEACHES:

I. That the apostles and Christ have been living on the earth since 1874 as invisible spirits in bodily form.

"1874 was the exact date of the beginning of the times of restitution and hence our Lord's return." (Vol. 2, pages 170, 171.)

"And while we therefore conclude that their resurrection is now an accomplished fact, and hence that they as well as the Lord are present in the earth, the fact we do not see them is no obstacle to faith when we remember that, like their Lord, they (the apostles) are now spirit beings, and, like Him, invisible to men." (Vol. 2, page 234.)

THE BIBLE:

1. Christ says no man, angel or even He knows the day or the hour (Mark 13: 32).

2. At Christ's return the dead Christians are to be raised and the living Christians are to be translated (I Thes. 4: 13-17).

3. NOTE: Mr. Russell and his "little flock" must have been overlooked.

II. That all worldly kingdoms will end in 1914 and the Church of Christ will be set up with Christ as Head.

"That the Lord must be present, and set up His kingdom, and exercise His great power so as to dash the nations to pieces as a potter's vessel. is then clearly fixed; for it is 'in the days of these kings'—before their overthrow—i. e., before A. D. 1914—that the God of heaven shall set up His kingdom." (Vol. II, page 170.)

THE BIBLE:

1. No man knows the day or hour (Mark 13: 32; Acts 1: 7).

2. 1914 is history and this did not come to pass.

III. That the harvest of the Gospel age was to end in 1914.

"Remember that the forty years of Jewish harvest ended Oct., A. D. 69, and was followed by the complete overthrow of that nation; and that likewise the forty years of the Gospel age harvest will end October, 1914, and that likewise the overthrow of Christendom, so-called, must be expected to immediately follow." (Vol. 2, page 245.)

THE BIBLE:

1. No man knows the day or hour (Mark 13: 32; Acts 1: 7).

2. 1914 is history and this did not happen.
Try the spirits to see if they are of God (I John 4: 1-3).

All quotations from the six volumes of Scripture Studies and the Watch-Tower.

CHRISTIAN SCIENCE

Early in the Nineteenth Century there appeared in Portland, Me., a mental healer, Dr. Quimby by name, who experimented in healing by mesmerism and hypnotism. From 1862 to 1865 he had a now noted patient—Mrs. Eddy—who in early womanhood attracted some attention as a mesmeric subject. Claiming to be healed by Dr. Quimby she became a student and advocate of his teachings. Dr. Quimby died in 1865 and in 1866 Mrs. Eddy had a timely revelation in which she claimed to have discovered the teachings of Christian Science. These teachings she incorporated in a book called Science and Health, and after copywriting it, sold it through many editions at a handsome revenue. A close comparison of Mrs. Eddy's Science and Health and Dr. Quimby's Science of Man will startle any reader by their similitude.

The first edition of the book appeared in 1875 and has gone through many changes and transpositions and with each change a rich harvest has been reaped from the sale of new editions. In 1876 Mrs. Eddy organized the first Christian Science Association with six pupils. In 1879 she organized the first Science Church in Boston with twenty-six members and herself as pastor. This became the Mother Church. All other churches organized are branches of the mother church. The membership of Christian Science Churches runs in ratio of about three women to every man.

Mrs. Eddy was married three times, once divorced and in many ways her career was a checkered one. She reaped handsomely from the revenue obtained from healings, lessons on healing, sale of Christian Science spoons, books and other remunerative methods. She died reported to be worth over three million dollars.

THE BIBLE

CHRISTIAN SCIENCE TEACHES:

I. That the Bible is impure.

"A moral and material sense stole into the divine record, with its own hue darkening to

110

some extent the inspired pages." (S. and H.,
139: 20-22.)

THE BIBLE:

(Prov. 30: 5; Rom. 3: 4; II Tim. 3: 16; II Peter
1: 21).

II. That some parts of the Bible are lies.

(Regarding Gen. 2: 7) "Is it the truth, or is
it a lie concerning man and God? It must be
a lie." (S. and H. 524: 25-27.)

THE BIBLE:
(Isa. 8: 20; Rom. 3: 4).

III. That the Bible does not contain all revelation.

"God had been graciously preparing me during
many years for the reception of this final revelation." (S. and H. 107: 3-5.)

THE BIBLE:
(Prov. 30: 6; Rev. 22: 18, 19.)

GOD

CHRISTIAN SCIENCE TEACHES:

I. That God is incorporeal, divine, supreme, infinite
mind, soul, spirit, principle, truth love, (S. and
H. 465: 8-10.)

"I knew the principle of all harmonious mind-
action to be God." (S. and H. 109: 16, 17.)

THE BIBLE:

(Gen. 1: 1-31; Heb. 1: 3.) God is a personality.

JESUS CHRIST

CHRISTIAN SCIENCE TEACHES:

I. That Christ is not God.

"Jesus Christ is NOT God, as Jesus Himself
declared, but is the Son of God. This declara-
tion of Jesus, understood, conflicts not at all
with another of His sayings: 'I and my Father
are one,' that is, one in quality, not in quantity.

111

As a drop of water is one with the ocean, a ray
of light one with the sun, even so God and man,
Father and Son, are one in being." (S. and H.
36: 12-8.)

THE BIBLE:

1. Christ is called God (Isa. 9: 6; John 20: 28;
Phil. 2: 5, 6; Heb. 1: 8).

II. That Jesus was not incarnated in the flesh.

"Those instructed in Christian Science have
reached the glorious perception that God isn't
the only author of man. The Virgin Mother
conceived this idea of God, and gave to her ideal
the name of Jesus." (S. and H. 29: 14-18.)
"Jesus was the offspring of Mary's self-con-
scious communion with God." (S. and H. 29:
32; 30: 1.)

THE BIBLE:

1. Jesus was incarnated in the flesh (Luke 1: 30,
31, 34, 35; John 1: 14).

III. That every spiritual idea is a child.

"When a new spiritual idea is born to earth the
prophetic Scripture of Isaiah is renewedly fulfilled, 'unto us a child is born.'" (S. and H.
109: 24-27.)

THE BIBLE:

1. Jesus coming fulfilling (Isa. 9: 6) said He had
flesh and bones (Luke 24: 39).

NOTE: Ideas do not have flesh and bones.

IV. That Christ is not a man, but an ideal truth.

"Christ is the ideal truth, that comes to heal
sickness and sin through Christian Science, and
attributes all power to God. Jesus is the name
of the man, who, more than all other men, has
presented Christ, the true idea of God, healing
the sick and sinning and destroying the power
of death. Jesus is the human man and Christ

112

is the divine idea; hence the duality of Jesus the Christ." (S. and H. 475: 10-17.)

"The Christ is incorporeal, spiritual." (332: 11, 12.)

THE BIBLE:

1. That Jesus and Christ are the same person and had a fleshly body (John 20. 31; Rom. 5: 8; I Cor. 15: 3; I Peter 1: 19; Eph. 2: 13-16).

2. That a man is a liar who denies Jesus and Christ are the same (I John 2: 22).

3. That he is a DECEIVER who does not confess that Jesus Christ is come in the flesh (II John 7).

V. That Christ did not actually die.

"They saw Him after His crucifixion and learned that He had not died." (46: 2, 3.)

"His disciples believed Jesus to be dead while He was hidden in the sepulchre, whereas He was alive." (44: 28, 29.)

"The (seeming) death of His Son." (45: 11, 12.)

THE BIBLE:

1. He actually died (John 19: 33; Rom. 5: 8; 14: 9; 15: 3).

VI. That the blood of Christ does not cleanse the sinner of sin.

"The material blood of Jesus was no more efficacious to cleanse from sin when it was shed on the accursed tree than when it was flowing in His veins as He went daily about His Father's business." (25: 6-9.)

NOTE: Since Jesus and Christ are the same person (see No. 4 above), then here is an admittance that He came in flesh and that blood coursed through His veins, which contradicts the statement that Christ did not come in the flesh.

113

THE BIBLE:

1. The Bible says we are cleansed of sin by Christ's blood (Rom. 5: 9; Col. 1: 20; Heb. 10: 4-12; I John 1: 7).

VII. That Christ did not physically rise from the dead.
"To accommodate Himself to immature ideas of spiritual power, for spirituality was possessed only in a limited degree even by His disciples, Jesus called the body, which by spiritual power He raised from the grave, 'flesh and bones.'" (313: 26-30.)

THE BIBLE:

1. Jesus said He physically rose from the dead (Luke 24: 39-43; John 20: 26-29).

VIII. That Jesus did not ascend in His physical body.
"The eternal Christ and the corporeal Jesus manifest in flesh, continued until the Master's ascension, when the human, material concept, or Jesus, disappeared, while the spiritual self, or Christ, continued to exist." (334: 14-17.)

THE BIB'E:

The Bible says Jesus did ascend into heaven (Luke 24: 50, 51; Acts 7: 55; 9: 5; Heb. 4: 14).

IX. That Jesus will not return in bodily form.
"The second appearing of Jesus is, unquestionably, the spiritual advent of the advancing idea of God as in Christian Science." (Retrospection and Introspection 70: 20-22.)

THE BIBLE:

1. The Bible says He will return in the same manner that He went (Acts 1: 11).

THE HOLY SPIRIT

CHRISTIAN SCIENCE TEACHES:

I. That the Holy Spirit is divine science.
"In the words of St. John: 'He shall give you another Comforter, that he may abide with you

forever.' This Comforter I understand to be divine science." ، (55: 27-29.)

"The science of being shows it to be impossible for Infinite Spirit or soul to be in a finite body." (309: 24, 25.)

The Bible:

1. Christ said He would send the Spirit (John 16: 13, 14).

2. Paul says the Spirit dwells in us (I Cor. 3: 16; 6: 19; II Tim. 1: 14).

THE TRINITY

Christian Science Teaches:

I. That there are not three persons in the one God-head.

"The theory of three persons in one God ('That is, a personal trinity or tri-unity) suggests poly-theism, rather than the one ever-present I Am." (256: 9-11.)

"The name, Elohim, is in the plural, but this plurality of Spirit does not imply more than one God, nor does it imply three persons in one." (515: 17-19.)

The Bible:

1. God said, "Let US make man in our image" (Gen. 1: 26).

2. Christ commanded baptism into three persons of the God-head (Matt. 28: 19).

3. Christ came in the express image of God's person (Heb. 1: 3).
   God, then, is a person, showing that the three in the God-head are persons.

THE DEVIL

Christian Science Teaches:

I. That the devil is a lie and an error.

"Devil . . . . a lie: error . . . . a belief in sin, sickness and death." (584: 17-19.)

"The beliefs of the human mind rob and enslave, and then impute this result to another illusive personification, named Satan." (187: 10-12.)

THE BIBLE:

1. The Bible says there is a devil (Rev. 12: 9, 12; Matt. 4: 11; Luke 22: 31).

2. Christ said the devil is a liar (John 8: 44).

SIN

CHRISTIAN SCIENCE TEACHES:

I. That it is impossible for a man to fall in sin.

"Never born and never dying, it was impossible for man, under the government of God in eternal science, to fall from his high estate." (258: 27-30.)

"The great spiritual fact must be brought out that man is, not shall be, perfect and immortal." (428: 22, 23.)

II. That sin is an illusion.

"Matter and its effects, sin, sickness and death are states of mortal mind which act, react, and then come to a stop . . . . they are not ideas. but illusions. (283: 8-11.)

THE BIBLE:

1. The Bible says that there is no man that does not sin (I Kings 8: 46).

2. Christ says men sin (Luke 7: 47).

3. The Holy Spirit is to reprove the world of sin (John 16: 8).

4. Paul says all have sinned and come short of the glory (Rom. 3: 23).

5. John, an apostle, says if we say we have no sin we lie and deceive ourselves (I John 1: 8, 9).
NOTE: Christian science, then, deceives and lies.

III. That to get rid of sin is to divest sin of any supposed reality.

"To get rid of sin through science, is to divest sin of any supposed mind or reality." (339: 28-30.)

THE BIBLE:
(Matt. 9: 6; Col. 2 13; Eph. 1: 7).

IV. That man can not sin.
"Man is incapable of sin." (475: 28.)
"Soul is the divine principle of man and never sins." (481: 28.)

THE BIBLE:
1. All have sinned and come short of the glory of God (I Kings 8: 46; Rom. 3: 23).

V. That there is no such thing as sickness, disease or pain.
"Matter and its effects, sin, sickness, and death, are states of mortal illusions." (285: 8, 9, 11.)
"Man is never sick." (393: 29.)
"There is no disease." (421: 18.)

THE BIBLE:
(Matt. 4: 24; Mark 6: 5; John 4: 46.)

VI. That growing old is an illusion.
"Decrepitude is not according to law nor is it a necessity of nature, but an illusion. (245: 30-31.)

THE BIBLE:
(Gen. 48: 10; Prov. 16: 31.)

VII. That there is no death.
"Jesus restored Lazarus by the understanding that Lazarus had never died." (75: 13-15.)
"Man is incapable of sin, sickness and death." (475: 28.)
"Death. An illusion." (584: 9.)

THE BIBLE:
1. Man has died from the beginning (Gen. 5: 1-5).

117

2. Jesus said PLAINLY, "Lazarus is dead" (John 11: 14).

3. It is appointed unto men once to die (Heb. 9: 27).

CHRISTIAN SCIENCE TEACHES:

I. That "until it is learned that generation rests on no sexual basis, let marriage continue." (Teaching 1893.)

"Until it is learned that God is the Father of all, let marriage continue." (Teaching in 1906.)

"Until it is learned that God is the Father of all, marriage will continue." 1917 (64: 26, 27.)

"Until time matures human growth, marriage and progeny will continue unprohibited in Christian Science." (Miscellaneous Writings 286: 6-8.)

"God created all through mind, and made all perfect and eternal. Where, then, is the necessity for recreation or procreation?" (205: 12-14.)

THE BIBLE:

1. God commanded man to multiply (Gen. 1: 26-28).

2. The Spirit spoke expressly that in the latter times some, who were seducing spirits, liars, servants of the devil, would depart from the faith and teach against marriage (I Tim. 4: 1-3).

DIVORCE

CHRISTIAN SCIENCE TEACHES:

I. That divorce is all right.

"I hereby state, in unmistakable language, the following statute in the morale of Christian Science: A man or woman having voluntarily entered into wedlock and accepted the claims of the marriage covenant, is held in Christian Science as morally bound to fulfill all the claims growing out of this contract, unless such claims

118

are relinquished by mutual consent of both parties, or this contract is legally dissolved." (Miscellaneous Writings 297: 18-25.)

THE BIBLE:

1. A man putting away his wife, except for fornication, and marrying another, commits adultery (Matt. 5: 31, 32; 19: 8, 9).

CHILDREN

CHRISTIAN SCIENCE TEACHES:

I. That children are spiritual thoughts and representations of life, truth and love.

"Children, the spiritual thoughts and representatives of life, truth and love. Sensual and moral beliefs; counterfeits of creation, whose better originals are God's thoughts, not in embryo, but in maturity; material suppositions of life, substance and intelligence, opposed to the science of being. (528: 28; 585: 4.)

THE BIBLE:
(Psa. 127: 3-5.)

CHRISTIAN SCIENCE SUBTRACTIONS AND SUBSTITUTIONS

CHRISTIAN SCIENCE SUBTRACTS:

I. Baptism.

THE BIBLE:

1. Christ commands it and promises salvation only to those who obey it (Matt. 28: 19, 20; Mark 16: 15, 16; Matt. 3: 13; Acts 2: 38; 8: 36-39; 22: 16; I Cor. 12: 13; Gal. 3: 27; I Peter 3: 21).

II. The Lord's Supper.

THE BIBLE:

1. The Bible commands the observance of the Lord's Supper weekly (Acts 2: 42; 20: 7; I Cor. 11: 23-29).

2. No life in us if we do not do this (John 6: 53).

119

III. The Scriptural plan of salvation.

THE BIBLE:

1. Faith in God and Jesus Christ as His Son (Heb. 11: 6; John 14: 1).
2. Repentance (Luke 13: 3; Acts 17: 30; II Peter 3: 9).
3. Confession of Christ (Matt. 10: 32, 33; Rom. 10: 9, 10).
4. Baptism (Matt. 28: 19, 20; Mark 16: 15, 16; John 3: 5; Rom. 6: 3-5; Gal. 3: 27; I Peter 3: 21).
5. Continuing in the apostles' teaching, and fellowship, breaking of bread and prayers (Acts 2: 42).
6. Adding of all the Christian graces (II Peter 1: 5-11).

CHRISTIAN SCIENCE SUBSTITUTES:

I. A name.

THE BIBLE:

1. Name of Church organization.
   (1.) Church of God (Acts 20. 28; I Cor. 1: 2).
   (2.) Church of the Living God (I Tim. 3: 15).
   (3.) Church of the First-born (Heb. 12: 23).
   (4.) Body of Christ (Eph. 4: 12; 5: 23; Col. I: 24).
   (5.) Church of Christ (Rom. 16: 16; Eph. 5: 23).
2. Name of church members.
   (1.) Disciples (Acts 11: 26).
   (2.) Saints (Phil. 1: 1).
   (3.) Brethren (I Cor. 15: 6).
   (4.) Christians (Acts 11: 26; 26: 28; I Peter 4: 16).

NOTE: The name Christian is preferable because the names, disciples, brethren, saints, etc., were common among the Jews, but the name,

Christian, is distinctly a new name (Isa. 62: 1, 2; Acts 11: 26). Again the members are married to Christ and should wear the name that shows marriage relationship (Rom. 7: 4).

II. Science and health for the Bible.

NOTE: How many times Science and Health contradicts the Scriptures is evident by all the preceding comparisons.

III. Mrs. Eddy's authority for Christ's authority.

THE BIBLE:

1. Christ said all authority is given unto HIM in heaven and earth. This is all inclusive (Matt. 28: 18).

2. Paul says let God be true and every man a liar (Rom. 3: 4).

NOTE: All quotations from Science and Health are taken from the 1917 edition.

SECTION III.

The Restoration Movement in the Light of Scripture

THE CHURCH OF CHRIST

The Church of Christ is the result of a movement beginning in the first decade of the Nineteenth Century, proposing to restore to the world the primitive order of the Church in the first century. Thomas and Alexander Campbell and Barton W. Stone were the principal figures in the inception of the movement, the first two beginning their work in Western Pennsylvania and the latter starting his labors in Kentucky and Tennessee.

On August 17, 1809, the "Christian Association of Washington, Pa.," was formed for the purpose of promoting simple, evangelical Christianity, free from all human opinions and inventions of men. The Association by no means considered itself a church, but was only an attempt to throw off the fetters of denominationalism and return to the simplicity of New Testament Christianity. The two groups united in 1831.

The history of the Church of Christ is unique in that, whereas all other movements since the days of Luther strove to reform the apostacies of the Roman Catholic Church, this movement went back of all decrees of the Roman Church to the practice of the church fresh from the hands of Christ's apostles. The Church, strictly speaking, claims to be neither Protestant nor Catholic, since neither of these divisions existed in the first century, but simply attempts to set up again on earth the Church established on Pentecost. Their whole appeal is to "speak where the Bible speaks, and to be silent where the Bible is silent," to have a "thus saith the Lord," either in express terms or by approved precedent. Its mottoes are:

No book but the Bible.
No creed but the Christ.
No name but the Divine.
No plea but the Gospel.
No basis of unity, but the Scriptural.
In essentials, unity.
In opinions, liberty.
In all things, charity.

The movement has grown rapidly uniting many people with denominational differences into one body, thus making peace.

TO BE SAVED AND STAY SAVED

THE CHURCH OF CHRIST TEACHES:

I.

That a man must have faith.

1. We get faith by hearing (Rom. 10: 13-17; Mark 16: 15, 16).
   NOTE: Faith is not miraculously given.
2. We must believe:
   (1.) In God (Heb. 11: 6).
   (2.) In Christ as the Son of God (John 14: 1).
   (3.) In the Gospel (Mark 1: 15; 16: 15, 16).
   (4.) In the works or miracles of Jesus (John 10: 38; 14: 11).
3. Faith alone will not save.
   (1.) A man having faith without works can not be saved (James 2: 14).
   (2.) Faith without works is dead (James 2: 17).
   (3.) If faith alone would save, then all the devils would be saved, for they believe (James 2: 19).
   NOTE: This would be universal salvation.
   (4.) Faith is made perfect by works (James 2: 22).

(5:) We are not justified by faith only (James 2: 24).

(6.) Faith without works is as dead as the body without the spirit (James 2: 26).

(7.) Faith only gives us power "to become" sons of God (John 1: 12).

(8.) Faith is "unto" righteousness (Rom. 10: 10).

II.

That a man must repent, which is a change of the will or the "right about face" of the soul.

1. NOTE: It is repent or perish (Luke 13: 3).
2. Repentance is the first command in the Christian dispensation (Acts 2: 38).
3. All men must repent (Acts 17: 30).
4. God's goodness leads men to repentance (Rom. 2: 4).
5. Repentance is part of the foundation of the Christian life (Heb. 6: 1).
6. God desires all men to repent (II Peter 3: 9).
7. Repentance is "unto" salvation (Acts 11: 18).

NOTE: Since there are sins of commission and omission a person in order to fully obey the act of repentance must not only repent of the sins he has committed, but he must also repent of the things he has left undone and do them. Therefore, if in the study of God's commands, he finds some he has not obeyed, he should repent of not having obeyed them and submit to them.

III.

That a man must confess Christ.

1. Reasons for making this confession.

(1.) We confess Christ for our salvation (Rom. 10: 10).

(2.) We confess Christ for the preacher's benefit (Acts 8: 37).

NOTE: That he may know we are a proper subject of baptism.

(3.) We confess Christ that He may confess us (Matt. 10: 32).

(4.) We confess Christ to glorify God (Phil. 2: 11).

2. Confession is "unto" salvation (Rom. 10: 10).

IV.

That a man must be baptized.

1. Baptism is commanded (Matt. 28: 19, 20; Mark 16: 15, 16; Acts 2: 38).

2. Baptism is into the name of the Father and of the Son and of the Holy Spirit (Matt. 28: 19).

3. Definition of Baptism.

(1.) Christ was baptized "in" Jordan and came "up out of" the water (Mark 1: 9, 10).

(2.) Christ called baptism " a birth" (John 3: 5).

(3.) Baptism is called a "going down into" and a "coming up out of" (Acts 8: 36-39).

(4.) Baptism is called a "washing" (Acts 22: 16).

(5.) Baptism is called a "burial" (Rom. 6: 4).

(6.) Baptism is called a "planting" (Rom. 6: 5).

(7.) Baptism is called a "resurrection" (Col. 2: 12).

(8.) Baptism is called a "washing of regeneration" (Titus 3: 5).

(9.) Every one knows what these terms mean. The English version makes the meaning plain. The word, baptize, comes from the Greek word, "Baptizo", meaning to dip, plunge or immerse.

4. Only ONE baptism (Eph. 4: 5).
   (1.) Paul, after calling baptism a burial, a planting, and a resurrection, says there is ONE baptism. He ought to know.
5. Baptism is essential to salvation.
   (1.) Baptism is to flee the wrath to come (Matt. 3: 7).
   (2.) Baptism is to fulfill all righteousness (Matt. 3: 14, 15).
   (3.) Baptism is a means by which heaven is opened to us (Matt. 3: 16). Heaven being opened to Christ in baptism pictures the fact that heaven is opened to us in baptism.
4. Baptism is to make us sons of God (Matt. 3: 17).

> NOTE: Christ was acknowledged as God's Son after He was baptized. Baptism being a birth (John 3: 5) makes us sons of God.

   (5.) Baptism is to please God (Matt. 3: 17).
   NOTE: God was pleased in Christ when He obeyed it.
   (6.) Baptism is to justify God (Luke 7: 29).
   (7.) Baptism is to accept the counsel of God (Luke 7: 30).
   (8.) Baptism is to manifest Christ to the world (John 1: 31).
   (9.) Baptism is for the remission of sins (Acts 2: 38).
   (10.) Baptism is in order to receive the gift of the Holy Spirit (Acts 2: 38).
   (11.) Baptism is to commemorate the burial of Christ (Rom. 6: 4).
   (12.) Baptism is to commemorate the resurrection of Christ (Col. 2: 12).
   (13.) Baptism is to get into the Church (I Cor. 12: 13).

(14.) Baptism is to get into Christ, therefore into the Church (Gal. 3: 27).

(15.) Baptism is to cleanse us (Eph. 5: 26).

(16.) Baptism is to save us (I Peter 3: 21; Mark 16: 15, 16).

(17.) NOTE: If a man can be saved without baptism then he can be saved by some way not laid down in the commission (Mark 16: 15, 16).

If a man can be saved without baptism, he can be saved without a Saviour (Gal. 3: 27).

If a man can be saved without baptism, Christ lied when He said, "Except a man be born of the water and the Spirit, he CAN NOT enter into the kingdom of God" (John 3: 5).

(18.) Baptism is "into" a Saviour or into a state of being saved (Gal. 3: 27).

V.

That one in Christ is married to Him.

1. Christ said He is the Bridegroom (Mark 2: 19).
2. John said Christ has a bride and is the bridegroom (John 3: 29).
3. We are married to Christ (Rom. 7: 4).
4. We are espoused to Christ as the one husband (II Cor. 11: 2).
5. Christ is the husband and the Church is His bride (Eph. 5: 23-33).
6. The marriage relationship described by John (Rev. 19: 7-9; Rev. 21: 1, 2, 9).

VI.

That we should wear Christ's name.

1. This fact pictured in Adam and His wife wearing the same name (Gen. 5: 2).

2. Adam was a figure of Christ (Rom. 5: 14; I Cor. 15: 45).

3. Adam's wife would be a figure of Christ's wife —the Church.

   NOTE: Adam and his wife wearing the same name pictures the fact that Christ and His wife, the Church, should wear the same name.

4. Prophesied that Christ's servants should wear a new name, given by the mouth of the Lord (Isa. 62: 1, 2).

5. Prophecy fulfilled.
   (1.) Salvation went out from Jerusalem (Acts 2: 1-47; Luke 24: 47).
   (2.) The Gentiles saw His righteousness (Acts 10: 1-48; 11: 1).
   (3.) When these two things came to pass the new name was given (Acts 11: 25, 26).
   (4.) NOTE: "C-H-R-I-S-T-I-A-N". "Ian" means "belonging to".

6. Agrippa knew the followers of Christ wore Christ's name (Acts 26: 28).

7. Peter said we are to suffer in the name, Christian (I Peter 4: 16).

8. We wear Christ's name in two worlds (Rev. 22: 4).

9. No salvation promised in any other name (Acts 4: 12).

VI.

That we should continue in the Apostles' doctrine (Acts 2: 42).

1. Doctrine means "teaching".

2. We must continue steadfastly in the Apostles' doctrine (Acts 2: 42).

3. We worship Christ in vain when we teach for

128

doctrine the commandments of men (Matt. 15:
9).

NOTE: This excludes all creeds, confessions of
faith and books of discipline.

4. We should mark and avoid those that cause
divisions contrary to the doctrine (Rom. 16: 17).

5. By preaching doctrine the preacher saves himself and those that hear him (I Tim. 4: 16).

6. All Scripture is profitable for doctrine (II Tim.
3: 16).

7. Baptism is part of the doctrine (Heb. 6: 2).

8. We are not to be carried about by strange doctrines (Heb. 13: 9).

9. We must not receive into our homes or bid God-
speed those who do not preach the doctrine of
Christ (II John 9. 10).

VIII.

That we must continue in the fellowship (Acts 2: 42).

1. We are to continue steadfastly in the fellowship
(Acts 2: 42).

2. Fellowship means:
   (1.) To give (Rom. 15: 26; II Cor. 8: 4; 9:
   13; Heb. 13: 16).
   (2.) To have partnership in the blessings of the
   death of Christ (I Cor. 10: 16).
   (3.) To have partnership in the strength and
   fellowship of the Holy Spirit (II Cor. 13:
   14).
   (4.) To have partnership in the sufferings of
   Christ (Phil. 3: 10).
   (5.) To have partnership in the blessings of the
   Gospel (Phil. 1: 5).
   (6.) To have partnership with the Father and
   the Son (I John 1: 3).

      (7.) The primary meaning here is "to give" (Acts 2: 44, 45; 4: 32-35).

      (8.) We are to give regularly (I Cor. 16: 1, 2).

IX.

That we are to break the bread (Acts 2: 42).

1. The institution is called.
    (1.) The breaking of bread (Acts 2: 42; 20: 7).
    (2.) The Communion (I Cor. 10: 16).
    (3.) The Lord's Supper (I Cor. 11: 20, 21).
2. Eating the shewbread weekly was a picture of our partaking of the Lord's Supper weekly (Lev. 24: 5, 9; Heb. 10: 1; Acts 20: 7).
3. The early church continued steadfastly in the breaking of bread (Acts 2: 42).
4. The early church broke the bread each first day of the week (Acts 20: 7), as they gave each first day (I Cor. 16: 1, 2).
5. Christ said there is no life in us if we do not commune (John 6: 53-58).
6. Communing unworthily makes us sickly (I Cor. 11: 30).
7. The communion is neither "open" nor "closed".
    (1.) Christ is the only Judge (John 5: 22).
    (2.) Christ commands us not to judge (Matt. 7: 1).
    (3.) To invite or debar is judging the invited fit or unfit.
    (4.) Man is to examine himself (I Cor. 11: 28).
8. Communion makes us one (I Cor. 10: 16, 17).

X.

That we must pray (Acts 2: 42).

1. We are to continue steadfastly in prayer (Acts 2: 42).

2. Prayer commanded (Mark 13: 33; Luke 21: 36; Rom. 12: 12; 1 Thes. 5: 17; I Tim. 2: 1, 2).

XI.

That we are to add virtue (II Peter 1: 5).

1. We are to be physically virtuous (Matt. 5: 27).
2. We are to be mentally virtuous (Matt. 5: 27, 28).
3. We are to be spiritually virtuous (II Cor. 11: 2).

XII.

That we are to add knowledge (II Peter 1: 5).

1. We are not to wait until we know all things before coming into the Church. Knowledge is added after coming in.

2. Christians study for three reasons.
    (1.) To have God's approval (II Tim. 2: 15).
    (2.) To be not ashamed (II Tim. 2: 15).
    (3.) To rightly divide the Word (II Tim. 2: 15).

XIII.

That we are to add temperance (II Peter 1: 6).

1. There are three kinds of intemperance.
    (1.) Eating too much (Gen. 3: 6; Eccl. 10: 16, 17).
    (2.) Drinking too much (Prov. 23: 21; I Cor. 6: 10).
    (3.) Thinking sin (Matt. 5: 27; Rom. 1: 21-31).
2. Temperance is one of the fruits of the Spirit (Gal. 5: 22, 23).

XIV.

That we are to add patience (II Tim. 1: 6).

1. We are to possess our souls in patience (Luke 21: 19).

2. Tribulation worketh patience (Rom. 5: 3).

3. We must run the Christian race with patience (Heb. 12: 1).

4. Patience leads to perfection (James 1: 4).

XV.

That we are to add Godliness (II Peter 1: 6).

1. The godly have the promises of two worlds (I Tim. 4: 8).

2. Godliness is a gradual growth (II Cor. 3: 18).

XVI.

That we are to add brotherly kindness (II Peter 1: 7).

1. We are to be kindly affectioned one toward another (Rom. 12: 10).

2. Kindness is a part of the Christian's garment (Col. 3: 12).

XVII.

That we are to add love (II Peter 1: 7).

1. We are to love:
    (1.) God (Matt. 22: 27).
    (2.) Christ (Eph. 6: 24).
    (3.) Neighbor (Col. 5: 14).
    (4.) One another (John 15: 12).
    (5.) Our enemies (Matt. 5: 44).
    (6.) The Brotherhood (I Peter 2: 17).

2. If we add all of these we reach home.
    (1.) They give us an abundant entrance into the everlasting kingdom (II Peter 1: 8-11).
    (2.) We will never fall if we do these things (II Peter 1: 10).

(3.) We are to work out our salvation with fear and trembling (Phil. 2: 12).

(4.) It is not which one of these must I do to be saved. We must obey them all.

(5.) Faith plus works plus grace saves us (Heb. 11: 6; James 2: 24; Eph. 2: 8).

SECTION IV.

Biblical Teachings

"THE BIBLE ON BAPTISM"

1. They were baptized of John "in" the River Jordan (Matt. 3: 6).
2. To obey baptism is to flee from the wrath to come (Matt. 3: 7).
3. John baptized "in" water, but Jesus was to baptize "in" the Holy Spirit and "in" fire (Matt. 3: 11). It is "in" in the Greek.
4. Jesus came from Galilee to the Jordan to be baptized of John (Matt. 3: 13).
5. John said he had need to be baptized of Christ (Matt. 3: 14).
6. Jesus, when He was baptized, "went up straightway out of the water" (Matt. 3: 16).

    NOTE: Could Jesus have gone up straightway out of the water if He had not gone down into the water?

7. Jesus asked Zebedee's sons if they were able to be baptized with the baptism He was baptized with (Matt. 20: 22).
8. Jesus said they would be baptized with the baptism He was baptized with (Matt. 20: 23).
9. The baptism of John, whence was it? from heaven or from men (Matt. 21: 25).
10. We are baptized into the name of the Father and of the Son and of the Holy Spirit (Matt. 28: 19).
11. John baptized in the wilderness and preached the baptism of repentance for the remission of sins (Mark 1: 4).

12. Many people were baptized of John in Jordan (Mark 1: 5).

13. John baptized "in" water, but Jesus was to baptize "in" the Holy Ghost (Mark 1: 8). It is "in" in the Greek.

14. Jesus came from Nazareth of Galilee and was baptized of John "in" Jordan (Mark 1: 9).

15. Jesus asked James and John if they were able to be baptized with the baptism He was baptized with (Mark 10: 38).

16. Jesus told James and John they would be baptized with the baptism He was baptized with (Mark 10: 39).

17. The baptism of John, was it from heaven or of men? (Mark 11: 30).

18. "He that believeth and is baptized shall be saved" (Mark 16: 16).

NOTE: It does not read, "He that believeth and is saved shall be baptized." Jesus said that we must be baptized to be saved. There will be just two classes in the day of Judgment—baptized believers and unbaptized disbelievers. One will be a saved class and the other a damned class?

19. John preached the baptism of repentance for the remission of sins (Luke 3: 3).

20. To obey baptism is to flee from the wrath to come (Luke 3: 7).

21. The publicans came to John to be baptized (Luke 3: 12).

22. John baptized "in" water, but Jesus was to baptize in the Holy Spirit and "in" fire (Luke 3: 16).

23. When all the people were baptized, Jesus also was baptized (Luke 3: 21).

24. The people justified God being baptized with the baptism of John (Luke 7: 29).

NOTE: If being baptized with the baptism of John justified God in their obeying that baptism, certainly

135

being baptized in Christian baptism would fulfill the same purpose in even a greater way.

25. "The Pharisees and lawyers rejected the counsel of God against themselves, being not baptized of him" (Luke 7: 30).

    NOTE: Likewise many worldly wise ones today reject the counsel of God by not obeying the command to be baptized.

26. Jesus said He had a baptism to be baptized with (Luke 12: 50).

27. "The baptism of · John, was it from heaven or of men?" (Luke 20: 4).

28. Those sent of the Pharisees asked John why he baptized (John 1: 25).

29. John said he baptized "in" water (John 1: 26). "In" in the Greek.

30. John was baptizing in Bethabara beyond Jordan (John 1: 28).

31. John came baptizing in water that he might manifest Christ to Israel (John 1: 31).

    NOTE: As John's baptism manifested Christ to Israel, Christian Baptism manifests Christ to the world.

32. John was sent to baptize in water and upon whom he saw the Spirit descending and remaining on him the same is he which should baptize with the Holy Ghost (John 1: 33).

33. Jesus called baptism a "birth" (John 3: 5).

    NOTE: To be born means to come out. No one ever heard of a child being born of a mother smaller than itself. Likewise to be born of the water requires a larger body of water than the one baptized.

    NOTE: Jesus said this under an oath. The word, "Verily", is from the Greek word, "Amen". Amen coming at the end of a sentence means, "So be it." That is why Amen is said at the end of a prayer. But "Amen" coming at the beginning of a sentence shows that every thing that follows is said under an "oath".

136

Jesus said under a double oath, "Verily, Verily, I say unto thee, Except a man be born of water and of the Spirit, he can not enter into the kingdom of God." Jesus ought to know.

34. Jesus tarried with His disciples in the land of Judea and baptized (John 3: 22).

35. John was baptizing in Aenon (name of a river) near to Salim, because there was much water there (John 3: 23).

    NOTE: The reason for John's baptizing there was because there was much water there. It takes much water to administer baptism.

36. Jesus baptized and all men came unto Him (John 3: 26).

37. Jesus made and baptized more disciples than John (John 4: 1).

38. Jesus Himself baptized not, but His disciples (John 4: 2).

39. Jesus went away beyond Jordan to the place where John at first baptized (John 10: 40).

40. Jesus told His apostles that John baptized in water, but they were to be baptized with the Holy Spirit not many days hence (Acts 1: 5).

41. A successor of an apostle must have companied with Jesus and His disciples from the baptism of John to the ascension of Christ (Acts 1: 22).

42. Peter commanded his hearers on Pentecost to repent and be baptized in the name of Jesus Christ for the remission of their sins (Acts 2: 38).

43. Those that gladly received Peter's word were baptized (Acts 2: 41).

44. Both men and women were baptized (Acts 8: 12).

45. Simon was baptized (Acts 8: 13).

46. They were baptized in the name of the Lord Jesus (Acts 8: 16).

47. The Eunuch asked, "See, here is water; what doth hinder me to be baptized?" (Acts 8: 36).

48. Both Philip and the Eunuch went down into the water and Philip baptized the Eunuch (Acts 8: 38).

49. Paul was baptized (Acts 9: 18).

50. Peter refers to the baptism which John preached (Acts 10: 37).

51. Can any forbid water that these should not be baptized? (Acts 10: 47).

52. Peter commanded Cornelius' household to be baptized (Acts 10: 48).

53. John baptized with water, but Christ baptized with the Holy Spirit (Acts 11: 16).

54. John preached before Christ's coming the baptism of repentance to all the people of Israel (Acts 13: 24).

55. Lydia and her household were baptized (Acts 16: 15).

56. The Jailor and his household were baptized the same hour of the night (Acts 16: 33).

57. Many Corinthians hearing believed and were baptized, among whom were Crispus and all his house (Acts 18: 8).

58. Apollos knew only John's baptism (Acts 18: 25).

59. Paul found certain disciples who had been baptized unto John's baptism (Acts 19: 3).

60. Paul said John baptized with the baptism of repentance and that as John baptized he made the people promise to believe on Christ.
    NOTE: As far as believing in Christ was concerned, John's disciples were unbelievers, but they were baptized into a covenant that they would believe on Christ when He came.

61. John's disciples had to be rebaptized. This time they were baptized in the name of the Lord Jesus (Acts 19: 5).

62. Paul commanded to be baptized (Acts 22: 16).

63. By being baptized into Christ, we are baptized into His death (Rom. 6: 3).

64. We are "buried" with Christ by baptism into death (Rom. 6: 4).

65. Baptism is called a planting (Rom. 6: 5).

66. Paul wanted to know if any of the Corinthians were baptized into him (I Cor. 1: 13).

67. Paul was thankful that he had baptized none save Crispus and Gaius (I Cor. 1: 14).

68. Paul didn't want any to think that he baptized in his own name (I Cor. 1: 15).

69. The only other baptism he remembered performing was the household of Stephanas (I Cor. 1: 16).

70. Christ sent Paul not to baptize, but to preach the Gospel (I Cor. 1: 17).

   NOTE: No doubt Paul had his helpers do the baptizing, just as Jesus had His disciples do the baptizing (John 4: 1, 2).

71. The Israelites were baptized into Moses in the cloud and in the sea (I Cor. 10: 2).

   NOTE: The Israelites had dry land for a floor when they passed through the Red Sea (Ex. 14: 22), congealed walls of water on either side of them (Ex. 14: 22; 15: 8) and the cloud as a covering (Psa. 105: 39).

   This baptism in which they were submerged is a picture of Christian baptism in which we are buried. The Israelites being baptized into Moses is a picture of people today being baptized into Christ. Paul said these things happened unto them for ensamples and are written for OUR admonition (I Cor. 10: 11).

72. By one Spirit are we all baptized into one body—the Church (I Cor. 12: 13; Col. 1: 18, 24).

73. If the Corinthians did not believe in the resurrection, Paul wants to know why they baptized for the dead (I Cor. 15: 29).

74. As many as have been baptized into Christ have put on Christ (Gal. 3: 27).

75. One Lord, one faith, ONE baptism (Eph. 4: 5).

76. We are sanctified and cleansed by the washing of the water (Eph. 5: 26).

77: We are buried with Christ in baptism and risen with Him (Col. 2: 12).

78. We are saved by the washing of regeneration (Titus 3: 5).

79. The doctrine of baptism is part of the Christian foundation (Heb. 6: 2).

80. Our bodies are washed with pure water (Heb. 10: 22).

81. Baptism saves us (I Peter 3: 21).

DEFINITIONS OF BAPTISM

1. Jesus was baptized "in" Jordan, "straightway coming up out of" the water (Mark 1: 9, 10).

2. John calls baptism a "birth" (John 3: 5).

3. John was baptizing in Aenon, near to Salem, because because there was MUCH water there (John 3: 23).

4. Baptism is a "going down into" and a "coming up out of" (Acts 8: 36-39).

5. Baptism is a "washing" (Acts 22: 16).

6. Baptism is a "burial" (Rom. 6: 4).

7. Baptism is a "planting" (Rom. 6: 5).

8. Baptism is a "resurrection" (Col. 2: 12).

9. Baptism is a "washing of regeneration" (Titus 3: 5).

10. There is ONE baptism (Eph. 4: 5).

REASONS FOR BEING BAPTIZED

1. To flee the coming wrath (Matt. 3: 7).

2. To fulfill all righteousness (Matt. 3: 15).

3. To have heaven opened unto us (Matt. 3: 16).
   NOTE: Heaven being opened to Jesus is a picture of heaven being opened to us.

4. To become a son of God (Matt. 3: 17). Baptism is a birth (John 3: 5).

5. To please God (Matt. 3: 17).

140

6. To justify God (Luke 7: 29).
7. To accept the counsel of God (Luke 7: 30).
8. To manifest Christ to the world (John 1: 31).
9. To have our sins remitted (Acts 2: 38).
10. To receive the Holy Spirit (Acts 2: 38).
11. To commemorate the burial of Christ (Rom. 6: 4).
12. To commemorate the resurrection of Christ (Col. 2: 12).
13. To get into the Church (I Cor. 12: 13; John 3: 5).
14. To get into Christ (Gal. 3: 27).
15. To be cleansed (Eph. 5: 26).
16. To be saved (I Peter 3: 21).

THE BIBLE ON SPRINKLING

1. Sprinkling of *ashes* toward heaven Ex. 9: 8).
2. Sprinkling of *ashes* toward heaven (Ex. 9: 10).
3. Sprinkling of *blood* on the altar (Ex. 24: 6).
4. Sprinkling of *blood* on the people (Ex. 24: 8).
   NOTE: A picture of Christ's *blood* sprinkled on us (I Peter 1: 2).
5. Sprinkling of *blood* on the altar (Ex. 29: 16).
6. Sprinkling of *blood* on the altar (Ex. 29: 20).
7. Sprinkling of *blood* and oil on Aaron and his sons (Ex. 29: 21).
8. Sprinkling of *blood* on the altar (Lev. 1: 5).
   NOTE: A picture of the *blood* of Christ sprinkled on the cross. He is the final sacrifice.
9. Sprinkling of *blood* on the altar (Lev. 1: 11).
10. Sprinkling of *blood* on the altar (Lev. 3: 2).
11. Sprinkling of *blood* on the altar (Lev. 3: 8).
12. Sprinkling of *blood* on the altar (Lev. 3: 13).
13. Sprinkling of *blood* seven times before the vail (Lev. 4: 6).
    NOTE: The temple vail was rent when Christ's *blood* was sprinkled on the cross.
14. Sprinkling of *blood* seven times before the vail (Lev. 4: 17).
15. Sprinkling of *blood* on the side of the altar (Lev. 5: 9).
16. Sprinkling of *blood* on garments (Lev. 6: 27).
17. Sprinkling of *blood* on the altar (Lev. 7: 2).
18. Sprinkling of *blood* on the peace offering (Lev. 7: 14).
19. Sprinkling of *oil* seven times upon the altar (Lev. 8: 11).
    NOTE: (Lev. 8: 10) says it was oil that was sprinkled.

20. Sprinkling of *blood* upon the altar round about (Lev. 8: 19).

21. Sprinkling of *blood* upon the altar round about (Lev. 8: 24).

22. Sprinkling of *blood* and *oil* upon Aaron and his sons (Lev. 8: 30).

23. Sprinkling of *blood* upon the altar (Lev. 9: 12).

24. Sprinkling of *blood* upon the altar (Lev. 9: 18).

   NOTE: The *blood* of the "peace-offering" sprinkled upon the altar pictured the *blood* of our "peace-offering" sprinkled on the cross.

25. Sprinkling of *blood* of a bird upon a leprous person (Lev. 14: 7).

   NOTE: The *blood* being sprinkled upon a leprous person pictured the *blood* of Christ cleansing a leprous soul.

26. Sprinkling of *oil* seven times before the Lord (Lev. 14: 16).

   NOTE: Sprinkling of *oil* typifies the Holy Spirit,

27. Sprinkling of *oil* seven times before the Lord (Lev. 14: 27).

28. Sprinkling of *blood* and *water* mixed upon a house (Lev. 14: 51).

   NOTE: This is the first mention of *water* and it was mixed with blood.

29. Sprinkling of *blood* upon the mercy seat (Lev. 16: 14).

30. Sprinkling of *blood* on the mercy seat (Lev. 16: 15).

31. Sprinkling of *blood* on the altar (Lev. 16: 19).

32. Sprinkling of *blood* upon the altar (Lev. 17: 6).

33. Sprinkling of the *water* of purifying on people (Num. 8: 7).

   NOTE: This water of purifying, called water of separation and clean water consisted of five ingredients: Ashes of a red heifer, ashes of cedar wood, ashes of hyssop, ashes of scarlet and running water (Num. 19: 1-17)

34. Sprinkling of *blood* seven times before the tabernacle (Num. 19: 4).

35. Sprinkling of *water* of separation (Num. 19: 13).

    NOTE: This water of separation consisted of five things. After being sprinkled with this mixture, which really made a lye, the unclean person was to bathe in water. The unclean person had to be sprinkled twice—on the third and seventh days (Num. 19: 1-17).

    NOTE: This sprinkling could have no reference to baptism because the unclean is to be sprinkled with the water of separation in order to cleanse his flesh, whereas baptism is not performed to put away the filth of the flesh (I Peter 3: 21).

36. Sprinkling of the *water* of *separation* upon the tent (Num. 19: 18), vessels and all vessels defiled.

37. Sprinkling of the *water* of *separation* on the unclean (Num. 19: 19).

    NOTE: The unclean person was to be sprinkled with the water of separation on the third and seventh day. His garments were to be washed and his body bathed in water on the seventh day.

38. Sprinkling of the *water* of *separation* upon the unclean (Num. 19: 20).

39. Sprinkling of the *water* of *separation* (Num. 19: 20).

    NOTE: This verse refers to the one who did the sprinkling.

40. Sprinkling of *Jezebel's blood* on the wall (II Kings 9: 33).

41. Sprinkling of the *blood* of the peace offering (II Kings 16: 13).

42. Sprinkling of the *blood* upon the altar (II Kings 16: 15).

43. Sprinkling of *blood* upon the altar (II Chron. 29: 22).

44. Sprinkling of *blood* (II Chron. 30: 16).

45. Sprinkling of the blood of the paschal lamb (II Chron 35: 11).

    NOTE: The sprinkling of the blood of the paschal

lamb is a picture of the sprinkling of the blood of our Paschal Lamb upon us (Heb. 10: 22; I Peter 1: 2).

46. Sprinkling of *dust* upon the head (Job 2: 12).

47. Sprinkling of many nations (Isa. 52: 15).
NOTE: In the Greek this word means "admire". But even if it meant sprinkle this does not refer to baptism, because it does not tell what part of the body is sprinkled or with what it is sprinkled. The New Testament only can enlighten us. (Heb. 10: 22 shows the heart is sprinkled and the body washed with pure water. (I Peter 1: 2) shows that it is *blood* that is sprinkled. In a spiritual way Christ's blood is sprinkled upon us.

48. Sprinkling of *blood* (Isa. 63: 2).

49. Sprinkling of *clean water* upon people (Ezek. 36: 25).

NOTE: Clean water, or water of separation consisted of five ingredients (Num. 19: 1-17).
Israel had been in captivity thirty years (Ezek. 1: 1), and when God brought them back to their own land (Ezek. 36: 24), God was going to sprinkle them with the water of cleansing in order to purify them from their uncleanness after being among the heathen.

50. Sprinkling of *blood* of bulls and goats (Heb. 9: 13, 14).

NOTE: This refers to sprinkling of the blood of the old Jewish sacrifices. The sprinkling of the blood upon Jewish altars pictured the sprinkling of Christ's blood.

51. Sprinkling of the *blood* mixed with *water, scarlet wool* and *hyssop* upon the book and people (Heb. 9: 19).

NOTE: This was a cleansing of the flesh and baptism is not to cleanse the flesh (I Peter 3: 21).

52. Sprinkling of *blood* upon the tabernacle and vessels (Heb. 9: 21).

53. Sprinkling of the *heart* from an evil conscience (Heb. 10: 22).

    NOTE: The body is to be washed with pure water.
54. Sprinkling of the *blood* upon the door posts (Heb. 11: 28).
55. Sprinkling of the *blood* of Jesus Christ (Heb. 12: 24).
56. Sprinkling of the *blood* of Jesus Christ (I Peter 1: 2).

SUMMARY

1. Ashes, blood, oil, scarlet wool, hyssop, ashes of a red heifer, ashes of cedar wood, dust and clean water are said to be sprinkled.
2. Nowhere in the Old or New Testament is water alone (nothing but water) ever said to be sprinkled upon any one or anything.
3. Baptism is done in the name of the Father and of the Son and of the Holy Spirit, but sprinkling was done in no name.
4. No reference on sprinkling even hints at baptism.
5. The great Scriptural commands of obedience to the Gospel are faith, repentance and baptism. Paul said: "Let us draw near with a true heart (faith) in full assurance of faith, having our hearts sprinkled from an evil conscience (repentance), and our bodies washed with pure water" (baptism) (Heb. 10: 22). NOTE: Baptism is a washing (Acts 22: 16; Titus 3: 5).

146

SANCTIFICATION
THINGS SANCTIFIED

Teachings of Scripture:

I. "A Day" (Gen. 2: 3).
1. The Character of the day not changed.
2. The seventh day was simply "set apart" from other days.
3. It belonged to God whether man so recognized it or not.

II. "The First-born" (Ex. 13: 1-2).
1. Character of the first-born of man or beast not changed.
2. They were "set apart" for God.
3. They belonged to God.

III. "A Mountain" (Ex. 19: 23).
1. Character of the mountain not changed.
2. The mountain was simply "set apart" for God.
3. It belonged to God.

IV. "An Altar (Ex. 40: 10).
1. Character of the altar not changed.
2. The altar was "set apart" for God's use.
3. It belonged to God.

V. "Vessels" (Ex. 40: 9).
1. Character of the vessels not changed.
2. The vessels were "set aside" for God's use.
3. They belonged to God.

VI. "The Tabernacle" (Ex. 29: 44).
1. Character of the tabernacle not changed.
2. The tabernacle was "set apart" for God's service.
3. It belonged to God.

VII. "Holy Things" (I Chron. 23: 13).
1. Their character not changed.

147

2. The holy things were "set apart" for the service of God.

NOTE: If sanctification meant to make holy, how could you make "holy things" holy?

3. They belonged to God.

VIII. "Jerusalem" (Matt. 4: 5). (Holy City.)

1. Character of Jerusalem not changed.

(1.) Though a holy city, Jerusalem had killed the prophets (Matt. 23: 37).

(2.) Jesus said no prophet could die out of Jerusalem (Luke 13: 33).

(3.) Though a holy city, Jerusalem killed Christ (Matt. 27: 1-50).

2. Jerusalem called the "Holy City" because it was set apart and there God put His temple and His name.

3. It belonged to God.

IX. "Gate of City" (Neh. 3: 1).

1. Character of the gate not changed.

2. The gate was "set apart".

3. It belonged to God.

X. "God" (Isa. 5: 16; I Peter 3: 15).

1. Character of God not changed—He is always good.

2. God is "set apart" in the hearts of the righteous.

3. He belongs to the righteous—he is "our Father."

XI. "God's name" (Ezek. 36: 23).

1. Character of His name not changed.

2. God's name is "set apart" as the only name of Deity.

3. To let the heathen know that His name belonged to Israel (Deut. 28: 10). God's name belongs to Christians.

XII. "Christ" (John 10: 36).

1. Character of Christ not changed.

2. Christ is "set apart" for His mission in the world.
3. Christ belongs to us as our Redeemer.

XIII. "Unbeliever by the Believer" (I Cor. 7: 14).
1. Character of the unbeliever is not changed.
2. The unbeliever is simply "set apart" to make the union holy.
3. He is party to that union.

HOW ARE WE SANCTIFIED?

1. Sanctified by the Word (John 17: 17; Eph. 5: 26).
2. Through the offering of the body of Christ (Heb. 10: 10; Heb. 13: 12).

ORDER OF SANCTIFICATION (I Cor. 6: 11)

1. We are washed (Matt. 28: 18, 20; Mark 16: 16; John 3: 5; Acts 2: 38; Acts 22: 16).
2. We are sanctified (Eph. 5: 26; II Tim. 2: 19-21).
3. We are justified—made righteous (Matt. 12: 36, 37; Rom. 3: 24; 5: 1, 9; 8: 33; Titus 3: 7).
4. Note: These three things not the same thing.

WHAT SANCTIFIED PEOPLE DID

1. Sanctified people described (I Cor. 1: 1-2).
2. They were contentious (I Cor. 1: 11-13).
   (1.) They were men worshipers.
   (2.) They were divided.
3. Sanctified people were babes and carnal (I Cor. 3: 1-6).
   (1.) There was envy, strife and divisions among them.
4. Sanctified people were puffed up "pouters" (I Cor. 4: 18, 19).
   (1.) They needed a thrashing, like a child (I Cor. 4: 21).
5. Sanctified people were the worst fornicators in the world (I Cor. 5: 1).

6. Sanctified folk were lawing and defrauding each other. There was not a wise man among them (I Cor. 6: 1-8).
7. These sanctified people were having domestic troubles (I Cor. 7: 1-5).
8. Sanctified people worshiped idols (I Cor. 8: 1-13).
9. Sanctified people didn't want to pay the preacher, but Paul showed them the preacher should be paid (I Cor. 9: 1-15).
10. Sanctified people were on the verge of falling (I Cor. 10: 1-12).
11. Sanctified people had turned the Lord's Supper into a drunken, heathen feast (I Cor. 11: 20-34).
12. Sanctified folk were wrangling over spiritual gifts (I Cor. 12: 1-31).
13. Sanctified people were even doubting the resurrection (I Cor. 15: 1-58).

SUMMARY

1. Same word is used in the Old and New Testaments to express the idea of sanctification.
2. Sanctification always means "to set apart" something or some one for God as His own peculiar property.
3. Sanctification is distinct from forgiveness of sin, or cleansing.
4. Sanctification is distinct from justification.
5. Sanctification is "objective" from one standpoint, in that God sets apart, and "subjective" from another angle, in that we are to live a separated life of holiness.
6. Sanctified people are not saved, but set apart.

DIVINE HEALING

The Manifestations of the Holy Spirit.

1. The Holy Spirit is given to Christ without measure (John 3: 34; Col. 1: 19).
2. The Holy Spirit is given to men by measure.
   (1.) There are diversities of gifts, differences of administration and diversities of operations (I Cor. 12: 4-6).
   (2.) There are three degress or manifestations of the Holy Spirit.
      a. Baptismal (Acts 1: 5; 2: 1-4).
      b. Laying on of hands of an apostle (Acts 8: 17).
      c. Ordinary (Acts 2: 38).
   (3.) All degrees called "gifts" (Acts 11: 17; Rom. 1: 11; Acts 2: 38).

I. *Baptism of the Holy Spirit.*

1. Only two cases of this manifestation.
   (1.) The twelve apostles received it (Acts 1: 1-5, 26; 2: 1-4).
   NOTE: The baptism of the Holy Spirit promised only to the twelve (Acts 1: 1-5), so the 120 did not receive it.
   (2.) The house of Cornelius received it (Acts 10: 44-48; 11: 15-17).
   NOTE: This was to convince the Jews that the Gentiles were accepted (Acts 11: 17, 18).
2. The baptismal degree gave the apostles power to perform all manner of miracles (Acts 5: 12-16).
   (1.) Jews from fifteen different nations heard the apostles speak in their own tongue (Acts 2: 4-12).
   (2.) The apostles healed the sick (Acts 5: 12-16).

       (3.) The apostles could raise the dead.
         a. Peter raised Dorcas (Acts 9: 36-42)
         b. Paul raised a young man (Acts 20: 8 10).
       (4.) These were signs of an apostle (II Cor. 12: 12).

II. *Laying on of Hands.*
   1. Only four cases of this.
       (1.) The seven deacons by the apostles (Acts 6: 6).
       (2.) The Samaritans by Peter and John (Acts 8: 14-18).
       (3.) The twelve Ephesians by Paul (Acts 19: 6, 7).
       (4.) Timothy by Paul's hands (II Tim. 1: 6).
   2. No one but an apostle could confer the Holy Spirit on another by the laying on of hands.
       (1.) Church of Rome not being founded by an apostle had no spiritual gifts and Paul longed to come unto them to impart unto them some spiritual gift (Rom. 1: 10, 11).
       (2.) A preacher who was not an apostle could not impart the Holy Spirit by the laying on of hands (Acts 8: 12-17).
       (3.) Those who had had apostle's hands laid on them could not impart the Holy Spirit to others (Acts 6: 6; 8: 12-17).
       (4.) The apostles alone could impart the Holy Spirit by the laying on of hands (Acts 6: 6; 8: 14-17; 19: 6; II Tim. 1: 6).

III. *General Gift of the Holy Spirit.*
   1. Promised to the obedient (John 14: 15-17; Acts 2: 38, 39; Acts 5: 32; Rom. 5: 5; I Thes. 4: 8; I John 3: 24).
   2. The Holy Spirit dwells in us.
       (1.) Paul says He dwells in us (Rom. 8: 9, 11; I Cor. 3: 16; 6: 19; II Tim. 1: 14).

<ol start="2" type="1">
<li>Holy Spirit given to the Gentiles (Acts. 15: 8).</li>
<li>The disciples were filled with the Holy Spirit (Acts 13: 52).</li>
<li>We receive the Holy Spirit by faith (Gal. 3: 2).</li>
<li>The Spirit in our hearts cries "Abba, Father" (Gal. 4: 6).</li>
<li>God gives us His Holy Spirit (I Thes. 4: 8).</li>
<li>We are partakers of the Holy Spirit (Heb. 6: 4).</li>
<li>The "Anointing" (Holy Spirit) abideth in us (I John 2: 27).</li>
<li>God gives to us His Spirit (I John 4: 13).</li>
<li>Sinners are not to have the Spirit (Jude 19).</li>
</ol>

3. We know we have the Holy Spirit by the fruits (Gal. 5: 22, 23).

IV. *The Miraculous Manifestations of the Holy Spirit Have Ceased.*

1. Purpose of miracles.

    (1.) To confirm the word Christ brought (John 14: 11).

    (2.) To confirm the word of the apostles (Mark 16: 20; Heb. 2: 3, 4).

    NOTE: - Christ was speaking to the apostles in (Mark 16: 15-19). The antecedent of "them" and "they" in verses 17-19 is the "them" in verses 14 and 15.

    (3.) NOTE: The word has now been confirmed by these signs. If such signs continued today, confusion would result. Either the Scriptures would be doubted or some new message would be believed.

    Those who usurp the signs of an apostle today are false apostles (II Cor. 11: 13;

12: 12) and they do not accept the Word of God as final, but believe in special revelations.

2 If one gift of the Holy Spirit ended, then all the other gifts have ended.

(1.) Gift of prophecy ended (I Cor. 13: 8; Rev. 22: 18-19).

(2.) Gift of knowledge ended (I Cor. 13: 8).

(3.) Gift of tongues ended (I Cor. 13: 8).

(4.) It was prophesied that miracles would last forty years (Micah 7: 15).
NOTE: The Israelites wandered forty years.

(5.) At the death of the apostles and those on whom they laid their hands miracles would naturally cease.

(6.) These helps of the early days of the Church were put away (I Cor. 13: 11) and now a "more excellent way" is provided in the completed New Testament (I Cor. 12: 31). The things which abide are "Faith, hope, love" (I Cor. 13: 13).

V *The Apostles Could not Always Perform Miracles.*

1. Paul did not heal Epaphroditus (Phil. 2: 25-27).

2. Paul left Trophimus at Miletum sick (II Tim. 4: 20).

3. Paul instead of healing Timothy told him to take a little wine for his stomach's sake (I Tim. 5: 23).

4. Reason why Paul did not heal these.

(1.) Apostles only performed miracles where it was necessary to establish the testimony they brought (I Cor. 14: 22; Rom. 1: 11; Mark 16: 20; Heb. 2: 3, 4).

5. As the New Testament writings increased the signs decreased.

6. Healing is not dependent on faith as some teach today.

   (1.) Church at Rome with a faith spoken of throughout the world (Rom. 1: 8) had no miraculous gifts (Rom. 1: 11).

   (2.) Timothy with unfeigned faith (II Tim. 1: 5) had to take medicine (I Tim. 5: 23).

VI. *Miracle Workers Today are of the Devil.*

1. The dragon, the devil (Rev. 12: 9) persecutes the woman, the Church (Rev. 12: 1-17).

2. The first beast. Political Rome, receives his power from the devil (Rev. 13: 1-10).

3. The second beast, Papal Rome, exercises all the power of the first beast, Political Rome (Rev. 13: 11, 12) and deceives people by working miracles (Rev. 13: 13, 14; 19: 20).

   NOTE: The book of Revelation is written in signs and symbols "sign-i-fied" (Rev. 1: 1) and the dragon is a symbol of the devil, the first beast of Political Rome and the second beast of Papal Rome. Papal Rome has always ridden on the beast—Political Rome. She is a religo-political organization. The Catholic Church has always claimed to work miracles, healing by means of relics, bones of saints, etc., deceiving the people thereby.

4. Denominational churches claiming to work miracles are like their mother. Catholic Church claims to be the mother of all churches (See her catechism). She is called the mother of harlots in (Rev. 17: 5).

5. People claiming to heal and perform miracles today get their power from the false prophet (Rev. 19: 20).

   (1.) The devil counterfeits apostles (II Cor. 11: 13-15).

   (2.) He uses some of the most sincere, prayerful and righteous people (II Cor. 11: 15).

155

<ul>
<li>(3.) People are thereby deceived.</li>
<li>(4.) Miracles are signs of an apostle (II Cor. 12: 12) and to claim to perform them today is usurping the signs of an apostle. Such are false apostles.</li>
</ul>

VII. *Jesus Will not Recognize Miracle Workers.*

1. He will call them "workers of iniquity" (Matt. 7: 23).
2. Working miracles is not doing the will of the Father (Matt. 7: 21, 22).
3. Many will try to save themselves by performing miracles (Matt. 7: 22).
4. Christ will tell such to depart from Him (Matt. 7: 23).

"APOSTLES"

I.

Meaning of the word, "Apostle".

1. An apostle is a "witness" (Luke 1: 2; 24: 33, 48; Acts 1: 15-26; 10: 41; I Cor. 15: 5; II Peter 1: 16; I John 1: 1).

II.

Choosing of the Apostles.

1. Chosen by Christ (John 6: 70; 15: 16; Acts 22: 14, 15).

2. Chosen by the will of God (Acts 1: 24; I Cor. 1: 1).

III.

Names of the Aposties.

1. Christ (Heb. 3: 1).
2. Peter
3. Andrew
4. James, Zebedee's son
5. John, his brother
6. Philip
7. Bartholomew
8. Thomas
9. Matthew
10. James, son of Alphæus
11. Thadæus
12. Simon, the Canaanite
13. Judas Iscariot
The original twelve found in (Matt. 10: 1-4)
14. Matthias (Acts 1: 15-26)
15. Paul (Acts 22: 14, 15; I Cor. 9: 1)
16. Barnabas Acts 14: 14)
17. James, the Lord's brother (Gal. 1: 19)

IV.

Qualifications of an Apostle.

1. An apostle must be a witness of Christ's resurrection (Luke 1: 2; 24: 33; Acts 1: 1-3, 19-22; 10: 39-41; I Cor. 9: 1; 15: 5, 7, 8; II Peter 1: 16; I John 1: 1).

2. An apostle's successor must not only have witnessed Christ's resurrection, but he must have

been with Christ from the baptism of John to
the Ascension of Christ (Acts 1: 21, 22).

V.

Powers of an Apostle.

   1. Apostles have power to bind and loose (Matt.
16: 19; Matt. 18: 18).

   2. Apostles have power to remit or retain sins
(John 20: 23).

   3. Apostles have power to heal all manner of sickness (Matt. 10: 1; Mark 16: 17, 18; Acts 5:
15; 19: 11, 12).

   4. Apostles have power to speak in tongues (Mark
16: 17; Acts 2: 4-11).

   5. Apostles could take up snakes without receiving
harm (Mark 16: 18; Acts 28: 1-6).

   6. Apostles could raise the dead (Acts 9: 36-43;
20: 9, 10).

VI.

Message of the Apostles.

   1. Their message was "The Word of God" (I
Thess. 2: 13).

   2. How the apostles' message was received.

      (1.) Jesus' message was from God (John 12:
49).

      (2.) Apostles received their message from
Christ (John 14: 26; 16: 13; Gal. 1: 1,
6-9).

      (3.) Apostles spoke by the direct authority of
Christ (I Cor. 5: 4; II Cor. 13: 3).

      (4.) Holy Spirit spoke through the apostles
(Matt. 10: 20; Luke 21: 15; John 14:
26; I Peter 1: 12; II Tim. 3: 16, 17).

      (5.) The words they spoke were "God-
breathed" (II Peter 3: 1, 2).

      (6.) Their words are to be kept in mind (II
Peter 3: 1, 2).

VII.

Signs of an Apostle.

1. Signs, wonders and mighty deeds (Acts 16: 17, 18; Acts 2: 43; 5: 12-16; Heb. 2: 3, 4; II Cor. 12: 12).

VIII

Importance of the Apostolic Office.

1. The Church is built upon the foundation of the apostles and prophets, Jesus being the chief corner stone (Eph. 2: 20).

2. The Church has only one foundation, of which the apostles are a part (I Cor. 3: 11; Eph. 2: 20).

IX.

Apostolic Succession.

1. Only one case of apostolic succession.—Matthias succeeded Judas (Acts 1: 15-26).

2. The successor of an apostle must have companied with Christ from the baptism of John to the ascension of Christ (Acts 1: 22, 22).

3. When James was beheaded they did not meet and select one to take his place as in the case of Judas (Acts 2: 15-26; 15: 1-29).

4. NOTE: None today could meet the requirements of an apostle or the successor to an apostle.

False Apostles.

1. False apostles are deceitful workers (II Cor. 11: 13-15).

2. Men today who claim to perform miracles are usurping the signs of an apostle (II Cor. 12: 12) and therefore are false apostles (II Cor. 11: 13-15).

3. Christ says He will not know such (Matt. 7: 21-23).

159

"WAS MATTHIAS ONE OF THE TWELVE APOSTLES?"

I.

Matthias was numbered with the elevn apostles (Acts 1: 26).

1. The names of the eleven given in (Acts 1: 11). These eleven names with Matthias' name make twelve.

2. *"Numbered with the eleven* apostles" is the same phraseology as "For he (Judas) *was numbered with* us (Acts 1: 17).

3. The antecedent of "us" in (Acts 1: 17) is the eleven, named by name in (Acts 1: 11).

4. Judas plus "us" (the eleven) equals twelve.

5. "He was numbered with the eleven apostles," then, means he (Mathias) and the eleven make twelve apostles.

II.

Not only was Matthias numbered with the eleven (making 12), but he received the Holy Spirit the same as the other eleven apostles (Acts 1: 26; 2: 1-4).

"They were *all* filled with the Holy Spirit."

III.

On the day of Pentecost Peter stood up with the eleven (Acts 2: 14).

1. NOTE: Some claim that this means Peter was included in the eleven when he is said to stand up with the eleven and that there were only eleven men standing.

2. "Peter standing up with the eleven" is the same phraseology as "Now when the even was come, he (Christ) sat down with the twelve" (Matt. 26: 20).

   Also: "And in the evening he cometh with the twelve" (Mark 14: 17).

160

NOTE: Who would ever think to say that Jesus was one of the twelve in the above references? Jesus, sitting down with the twelve, made thirteen men sitting. This is proved beyond successful contradiction in another passage refering to the same incident.

"And when the hour was come, he sat down, and the twelve apostles with him" (Luke 22: 14).

3. Then since the phraseology is identically the same, "Peter standing up with the eleven" means there were twelve men standing. Peter was not included in the eleven, but was a twelfth man.

IV.

The apostolic college was spoken of as having twelve apostles after the choosing of Matthias (Acts 6: 2).

1. NOTE: This was before Paul was converted and chosen as an apostle (Acts 9: 1-31).

2. After Paul was converted he was brought to the twelve apostles (Acts 6: 2; 9: 27). A distinction is here made between Paul and the apostles.

V.

The Choosing of Matthias fulfills prophecy.

1. Prophesied in Psalms that another should take Judas' office (Psa. 69: 25; 109: 8).

2. This prophecy was spoken by the Holy Spirit through the mouth of David (Acts 1: 16).

3. Peter says the choosing of Matthias to take Judas' place fulfills this prophecy (Acts 1: 16, 20).

VI.

Qualifications of an apostle's successor.

1. He must be a man who had companied with the apostles all the time the Lord went in and out

among them from the baptism of John to the ascension of Jesus (Acts 1: 21, 22; 10: 39-41).

2. Matthias and Barnabas fulfilled these requirements and were eligible for selection to the apostolic college.

VII.

Matthias' choice was an answer to prayer.

- 1. Jesus had promised, even before He had promised the Holy Spirit to the apostles, that He would answer any prayer they asked (John 14: 13, 14).

NOTE: The answering of their prayer was not conditioned upon their first having received the Holy Spirit.

2. The eleven apostles prayed for the Lord to show which of the two eligible ones God *had* chosen to take the place of Judas' apostleship (Acts 1: 24, 25).

NOTE: (1.) The apostles themselves did not choose Matthias, but prayed God by the means of the casting of the lot to show which one He had chosen.

(2.) Some have objected to this as gambling, but had they arbitrarily chosen one man without casting lots "they" would have been doing the choosing.

(3.) Some object to this method, but God answered the prayer of Abraham's servant in the selection of a wife for Isaac by a method stipulated by Abraham's servant (Gen. 24: 1-27).

3. Luke writing by inspiration and long after this event, expresses final judgment in the matter.
NOTE: It can not be too well noted that no New Testament writer ever questions the authenticity of Matthias being included in the apostolic college of twelve.

NOTE: Some have thought that because Paul

states that he was chosen by "the will of God" (II Tim. 1: 1) he was claiming to be one of the twelve and the rightful successor to Judas. But Paul was not defending himself as a "successor to any apostle", but simply proving his apostleship.

VIII.

The choosing of Matthias fulfilled another prophecy—one that Jesus made (Matt. 19: 28).

1. Jesus prophesied that the apostles were to sit on twelve thrones (Matt. 19: 28).

2. They were to sit on these thrones in the regeneration (Matt. 19: 28).

   NOTE: 1. Regeneration is the renovation of the soul by a washing and gift of the Holy Spirit (John 3: 5; Titus 3: 5).

   2. Regeneration began on Pentecost (Acts 2: 38, 39).

3. They were to sit on these twelve thrones when Jesus sat on the throne of His glory (Matt. 19: 28).

   (1.) Peter, speaking on Pentecost, said that Christ was then sitting on the throne of His glory (Acts 2: 22-36).

4. Matthias had to be selected to fill the place of Judas in time for the day of Pentecost—the beginning of regeneration, or else one of the twelve thrones would have been unoccupied.

   (1.) That is why Peter said, "This Scripture must needs have been fulfilled" (Acts 1: 16).

5. These twelve were to judge the twelve tribes of Israel—the Jews (Matt. 19: 28).

   NOTE: On the day of Pentecost the hearers consisted of Jews out of every nation under heaven (Acts 2: 5).

Paul's apostolate was a special one to the Gentiles.

1. Proof (Acts 9: 15; 26: 14, 15, 21; I Tim. 2: 7; II Tim. 1: 11).

2. Paul distinguishes between his apostleship and that of the other apostles.

    (1.) Paul was an apostle to the uncircumcision —the Gentile (Gal. 2: 7-9).

    (2.) Peter, who was one of the twelve, was an apostle to the circumcision—the Jew (Gal. 2: 7-9).

    (3.) This would make Paul ineligible to sit on one of the twelve thrones judging the twelve of Israel, for his apostleship was a special one to the Gentiles.

3. Paul, though on equality with the other apostles (II Cor. 11: 5; 12: 11; Gal. 2: 16), never once included himself among the twelve (I Cor. 15: 5-9).

4. Paul, to the contrary, segregates himself from the twelve (I Cor. 15: 5-9).

    NOTE: (1.) "The twelve" here is the official title.

    (2.) When Paul spoke in (I Cor. 15: 5) of "the twelve", he is speaking of the time following Christ's resurrection. From that time until Christ's ascension, we know there were only eleven apostles (Matt. 28: 17; Mark 16: 14; Luke 24: 33-36), but Paul, writing at a later date and in the light of the choosing of Matthias soon after Christ's ascension, spoke of the twelve, for though Matthias was not yet chosen during the period referred to by Paul, yet he was a witness like the eleven of Christ's life, death and resurrection (Acts 1: 15-23), and could very properly be the missing one to make up the twelve.

(3.) Paul could not have become a successor of Judas, for while he had the qualification of an apostle, having witnessed Jesus' resurrection (I Cor. 9: 1), he lacked the proper credentials necessary to become a successor to an apostle, that of having companied with them from the baptism of John to Christ's ascension (Acts 1: 15-23).

5. NOTE: It is strange that some should claim Paul to be the rightful successor to Judas to sit on one of the twelve thrones when Paul never claimed that himself. Such claim more for Paul that he ever claimed himself.

"MARRIAGE"

I. *Bad marriages were the cause of God's first Grief.*

1. The sons of God, good men, married "fair" daughters of men (Gen. 6: 1, 2).

2. There were only two families in the age before the flood.
   (1.) The sons of God (Gen. 4: 25; 5: 3-32).
   (2.) The sons of men (Gen. 4: 9-23).

3. The descendants of Seth were called by the name of the Lord (Gen. 4: 25, 26).
   (1.) This is not true of the descendants of Cain.
   (2.) Servants of God in all ages are called sons of God (Job 1: 6; Hos. 1: 10; I John 3: 2).

4. The character of Seth's descendants proves that they were the sons of God (Gen. 5: 3-32; Gen. 6: 9; 7: 1).

5. The character of Cain's descendants proves that they were not the sons of God, but the sons of men.
   (1.) Cain's sons were murderers and polygamists (Gen. 4: 17-24).

6. God prepared to withdraw His Spirit (Gen. 6: 3).

7. Bad marriages resulted in much wickedness (Gen. 6: 1-5).

8. The flood resulted from these bad marriages (Gen. 6: 1-7; 7: 6).

II. *Christ says the cause of the flood was bad marriages.*

1. They were eating in disbelief (Rom. 14: 23; I Tim. 4: 1-5).

2. They were drinking in disbelief (Matt. 24: 38; Rom. 14: 23).

3. They were marrying—bad marriages (Matt. 24: 39).

4. They were giving in marriage—bad marriages (Matt. 24: 38; Luke 17: 26-29).

NOTE: It is not wicked to marry, but wicked to enter into bad marriages.

5. Death caught such unawares (Matt. 24: 39).

6. Unbelief and bad marriages will be the cause of the final punishment (Matt. 24: 37-39).

III. *Bad marriages were not allowed among the Jews.*

1. Israel would not allow Dinah to marry a Hivite (Gen. 34: 30, 31).

2. Israel was not allowed to marry Gentiles (Deut. 7: 1-4).

3. A Jew was not even allowed to marry out of his tribe (Num. 36: 1-13).

IV. *Christians should marry Christians.*

1. Christian widows must marry only Christians (I Cor. 7: 39).

NOTE: If Christian widows have no right to marry any except Christians, then the same is true of Christian maidens.

2. If Christians have no Scriptural right to marry any except Christians, it is sure that to do otherwise means to live in spiritual adultery.

3. We are commanded not to be yoked with unbelievers (II Cor. 6: 14-18).

4. We are to come out and be separate (II Cor. 6: 14-18; Rev. 18: 4).

5. If the Jew had no right to marry out of his tribe, Christians have no right to marry spiritual counterfeits and concubines.

DIVORCE

I.

Old Testament Divorce.
   1. Who might be divorced.
      (1.) Bought wife (Ex. 21: 7-10).
         Condition: "Not pleasing to him."
      (2.) Captive wife (Deut. 21: 10-14).
         Condition: "No delight in her."
      (3.) Unclean wife (Deut. 24: 1-4).
         Condition: "Uncleanliness."
      (4.) Strange or heathen wife (Ezra 10: 1-16).
         Condition: "Causing idolatry."
         (1.) NOTE: A Hebrew could not marry
            his wife again after divorcing her, if
            she married another man, even
            though he were dead or she were
            divorced from him.

II.

The Lord hated Divorce (Mal. 2: 14-16).

III.

Why Moses gave divorces.
   I. Because of the hardness of their hearts (Matt.
      19: 7-9).

IV.

New Testament Divorce.
   1. Reasons for divorce.
      (1.) For fornication (Matt. 5: 31, 32).
      (2.) When the unbeliever deserts a believer (I
         Cor. 7: 10-16).

V.

What God joins together let no man put asunder.
   1. God does the joining, man can not sever (Matt.
      19: 7-9).

VI.

Good people may be divorced from God.

1. God was married to Israel (Jer. 3: 14).
2. But God divorced Israel (Hosea 1: 1-4, 6, 8, 9).
3. We, as Christians, are married to Christ (Rom. 7: 4; John 3: 29).
4. We can become divorced from Him by falling from grace (Heb. 6: 1-6; Heb. 10: 26).

WITHDRAWING FROM A CHURCH MEMBER

1. How to deal with a brother who has trespassed against you (Matt. 18: 15-17).

2. Those who cause divisions are to be avoided (Rom. 16: 17).

3. We are not to associate or eat with fornicators, idolaters, railers, drunkards or extortioners (I Cor. 5: 1-13).
    (1.) Such a one is to be delivered to the devil (I Cor. 5: 5).
    (2.) This should be done to save his spirit (Zech. 3: 1-4; Psa. 109: 6).
    (3.) Paul delivered such to Satan (I Tim. 1: 19-20).
    (4.) Paul had a messenger of Satan to buffet him (II Cor. 12: 7-10).

4. We are to withdraw ourselves from all that walk disorderly and who have not Paul's teaching (II Thess. 3: 6).

5. We are to withdraw from and have no company with the man who obeys not the doctrine of Paul (II Thess. 3: 14, 15).

6. We are to reject a heretic after the first and second admonition (Titus 3: 10).

7. A man who consents not to wholesome words, the words of our Lord Jesus Christ, and to the doctrine, is to be withdrawn from (I Tim. 6: 3-5; II John 9-11).

8. They are not to be thrown out of the church, however.
    (1.) God hath committed all judgment to the Son (John 5: 22).
    (2.) Christ forbade us judging (Matt. 7: 1).
    (3.) NOTE: To judge a man and to throw him out of of the church would be doing what God Almighty will not do and what Christ told us not to do.
    (4.) We are to let the good and bad live together until judgment (Matt. 13: 24-30).
    (5.) God does the adding (Acts 2: 47).

(6.) God does the subtracting (John 15: 2).

NOTE: The branches represent individual members (John 15: 5). The unfruitful branches are taken away by God. The branch is still a branch, but severed and therefore a dead branch.

9. A member can not turn himself out.

(1.) He is born into God's kingdom (John 3: 5).

(2.) He is like a son born into his father's family in the flesh.

(a.) Does not matter how wicked a son may become, he is still his father's son.

(3.) So in the spiritual realm, a man born into the kingdom, though he become a profligate sinner, is still a son.

(4.) But God can disinherit him.

THE TIME WE HAVE TO OBEY THE GOSPEL

THE WORLD TEACHES:

I. That God has not set a definite time in which a man
must obey the Gospel after hearing it.
NOTE: It is a common conception held by the
majority of people that, though a man may have
come to a full realization of the requirements of
the Gospel upon him, he has plenty of time to
accept and many chances to obey it. A great
many preachers tell people to take their time and
think the matter over.

THE BIBLE:

I. Time Christ gave a man to follow Him (Luke 9:
59-62).
1. Christ put His finger on tender spots.
(1.) Not even burying a dead father or bidding
friends farewell were sufficient reasons for
delaying to follow Christ.
(2.) These were supreme tests.
2. Christ gave them no time whatsoever—they
were to follow Him immediately.
3. Christ knew if they turned back, even for these
seemingly good reasons, it would become harder,
each delaying moment for them to follow Him
and the chances were that they would never
obey Him.

II. Paul, writing by inspiration, said: "Now is the
accepted time; behold, now is the day of salvation" (II Cor. 6: 2).
NOTE: Paul was quoting prophecy which was
written by inspiration (II Peter 1: 21).

III. Holy Spirit, through Paul, said today is the day
(Heb. 4 · 7).
1. God has limited the time.
2. God has set a certain day.

172

3. The Holy Spirit said "Today" twice.

4. The day a man accepts he must obey and not harden his heart.

    (1.) A man must harden his heart to delay and the more he delays the more hardened his heart becomes, until he gets to where he can not obey at all.

IV. Time Paul gave his hearers to obey the Gospel.

  1. Paul at Antioch of Pisidia (Acts 13: 44-46).

    (1.) He preached just once.

    (2.) When they refused, Paul turned from them.

    (3.) It didn't make any difference what reason they gave.

      a. They might have said, "If the Gentiles have anything to do with this, count us out."

      b. They might have said, "We are not fully convinced."

    (4.) This shows there is no legitimate reason to be given for delaying and that we must obey the day we hear.

  2. Paul at Corinth (Acts 18: 5, 6).

    (1.) He preached just once.

    (2.) When they refused Paul left them.

    (3.) Paul had discharged his duty and said: "Your blood be on your own heads; I am clean."

    (4.) There were too many who would obey, for Paul to waste precious time on those who delayed.

V. The mysteries of the Gospel being revealed, the world is left without excuse (Rom. 1: 20; I Cor. 2: 7-10).

  1. The plan of salvation is so plain that a man is left without excuse.

VI. The Scriptures record only two men who asked for more time.

    1. Felix (Acts 24: 25).

        (1.) Felix asked for a more convenient time.

        (2.) The convenient time never came.

    2. Agrippa (Acts 26: 28).

        (1.) Agrippa was almost persuaded to become a Christian.

        (2.) According to history, Agrippa lost favor with the Emperor at Rome and was banished to Gaul, where he died in exile. He never became a Christian.

    3. The Holy Spirit has recorded these two examples to warn men that the Gospel must be obeyed when heard.

VII. In every case of New Testament conversion all who obeyed the Gospel did it the day they heard.

    1. The Pentecostians (Acts 2: 1-47).

        (1.) They obeyed the same day they heard (Acts 2: 41).

    2. The five thousand (Acts 4: 1-3).

        (1.) The context shows they accepted the day they heard.

    3. The Samaritans (Acts 8: 5-12).

        (1.) Hearing Philip, they believed and obeyed (Acts 8: 12).

    4. The Eunuch (Acts 8: 26-40).

        (1.) The Eunuch obeyed the hour he heard (Acts 8: 36-39).

        (2.) The Eunuch might have said, "I have never heard of Jesus before, I have never seen this Scripture just this way before; let me think about this a while."

        (3.) This shows that the preacher is not to even wait until the regular assembly of the church, but teach and baptize anywhere at any time.

5. Paul (Acts 9: 1-18).

    (1.) While Paul experienced this miraculous appearance of Christ on the way down to Damascus in order to be a witness of Christ's resurrection and thereby become an apostle, he was not told what to do to complete obedience until after three days (Acts 9: 6, 9-18).

    (2.) Paul obeyed the moment he was told what he had to do.

6. Cornelius (Acts 10: 1-48).

    (1.) Cornelius obeyed the day he heard from Peter what he had to do (Acts 10: 24-48).

7. Lydia (Acts 16: 13-15).

    (2.) The context indicates that Lydia obeyed as soon as she had heard.

8. The Philippian Jailor (Acts 16: 24-34).

    (1.) The Jailor and his household were baptized "the same hour of the night."

    (2.) They all were baptized "straightway".

9. John's disciples (Acts 19: 1-5).

    (1.) When they heard this they were baptized (Acts 19: 5).

VIII. To know and not obey is sin (James 4: 17).

1. Before a man knows he could not commit this sin.

2. After knowing, if a man does not obey he begins to commit a sin he never could have committed before.

3. To refuse to obey after receiving the knowledge of the truth is a wilful sin (Heb. 10: 26).

IX. God deludes those who do not obey the truth that they might be saved (II Thess. 2: 10-12).

1. Paul identifies the truth he is talking about—the truth which saves (II Thess. 2: 10).

2. It makes no difference what causes a man to refuse the truth (II Thess. 2: 10).

   NOTE: It makes no difference what manner of deceiveableness of unrighteousness causes a man to delay.

3. Salvation is blood bought (Acts 20: 28; I Cor. 6: 20).

4. There are too many who have never heard to waste time with those who refuse to receive the truth the moment they know it.

   (1.) Christ said, "Give not that which is holy unto the dogs" (Matt. 7: 6).

   (2.) Christ said, "Cast not your pearls before swine" (Matt. 7: 6).

5. God deludes a man for not receiving the truth which saves (II Thess. 2: 11).

   (1.) God first gives a man a chance to receive it (II Thess. 2: 10).

   (2.) When a man refuses, God sends strong delusion (II Thes. 2: 11).

   (3.) This delusion causes them to go on believing a lie.

   NOTE: a. They go on believing they are all right, but they are believing a lie. Many people after hearing the truth refuse to obey and go on thinking they are all right.

   b. God sends a lying spirit to those who reject Him (I Kings 22: 22).

   (4.) They are deceived (II Thess. 2: 12).

X. To refuse to obey the truth is the unpardonable sin (Matt. 12: 31, 32).

1. The Holy Spirit directed the writing of the Scriptures (Acts 1: 1, 2; II Peter 1: 21).

2. The Holy Spirit has revealed the plan of salvation through the Scriptures (I Cor. 2: 7-14).

3. To refuse to obey the truth as revealed by the Holy Spirit is rejecting the Holy Spirit.

XI. There is no second chance promised either in this life or after death.

1. God has not promised salvation to a man who obeys on a second hearing after he has once heard and fully understood (II Cor. 6: 2).

2. Christ showed that a man who has heard in this life has no second chance after death (Luke 16: 19-31).

NOTE: The world says, "Take your time and think it over." The Bible says, "Today, if ye hear his voice, harden not your hearts."

Only the judgment will reveal how many souls have been lost because some preacher told them to take their time and think it over. The blood of such will be upon that preacher's soul.

CONFIRMATION

I. Confirmation is of Roman Catholic Origin.

1. "Confirmation is a Catholic Sacrament." Ex. of C. C. P. 52.

2. "The Catholic Church has always held that Confirmation is one of the Seven Sacraments, the God-given channels by which His grace is brought to our souls through the ministry of His church. Ex. of C. C., P. 53.

3. Confirmation is "administered to us when we have come to the age of reason and after long and thorough preparation and is a sacrament of the church through which grace is conferred on baptized persons strengthening them for the duty of professing Christian faith." Ex. of C. C., P. 52.

4. "The Sacrament is generally administered among us when the candidate is about twelve or thirteen years of age; but this is by no means an ancient or universal practice. In the Oriental churches it is usually conferred immediately after baptism and this was the rule in all parts of the world until the thirteenth century. In fact, the prompt confirming of newly-baptized children was strictly enjoined, and penalties were prescribed for parents who neglected it. But gradually it was seen to be preferable to defer this sacrament (which is not necessary for salvation) to an age when it could be received 'with knowledge and free will.'" Ex. of C. C., P. 55.

THE BIBLE:

1. People in New Testament times were taught before and not after baptism (Matt. 28: 19, 20; Mark 16: 15, 16; Acts 2: 1-47; Acts 8: 26-39; Acts 16: 29-33; Acts 18: 8).

2. Since Confirmation is of Catholic origin (the Catholic authorities so claiming it) and the

Catholic Church is not to be found in the Scriptures, either in name or in practice, then it naturally and logically follows that confirmation is unscriptural.

3. Since confirmation, according to Catholic authorities, is not necessary to salvation, then it should not be practiced. To impose this practice upon any one is forcing them to conform to a nonessential.

II. Confirmation is based on Tradition and not on Scripture.

1. There is no mention in the Gospels of such an institution, but according to "tradition" and the general opinion of the doctors of the church, it took place during the forty days after the resurrection of our Saviour." Ex. of C. C., P. 53.

THE BIBLE:

1. All the Scriptures which cover the forty days Christ was on earth between His resurrection and the ascension are to be found in the following passages and there is no mention made of the institution known as confirmation: (Matt. 28: 1-20; Mark 16: 1-20; Luke 24: 1-51; John 20: 1-31; 21: 1-25; Acts 1: 1-9; I Cor. 15: 1-8).

III. Confirmation, as practiced by Protestants, is a borrowing from the Roman Catholic Church.

"Confirmation is a Catholic Sacrament. It is true that it exists in the schismatic churches of the east, which were originally members of the true church and have preserved most of her teachings; but the protestant sects have always denied the sacramental nature of confirmation. Some reject it altogether; others, such as the Episcopalians, retain an imitation of it—a ceremony which they call Confirmation, but which they hold to be merely a rite and not a sacrament." Ex. of C. C., P. 52.

1. The protestant churches being children of the Mother of Harlots, naturally resemble their mother (Rev. 17: 1-18).

   This woman here represents the Catholic Church because:

1. She is a city on seven hills (Rev. 17: 9, 18).

2. NOTE: Rome, the center of Catholicism, is built on the seven Palatine hills.

3. She sits on many waters—peoples, multitudes, nations, and tongues (Rev. 17: 1, 15).

   NOTE: This is true because of the fact that the Catholic Church is a Religious-Political organization and seeks to rule the world politically and spiritually.

4. She has made the world drunk with the wine of her spiritual fornication (Rev. 17: 1, 2).

   NOTE: Every church that came from her and brought over some of her teachings and false doctrines is to that extent drunk with the wine of her spiritual fornication.

5. She is called the Mother of Harlots and in her catechism she teaches that she is the mother of all churches.

6. Confirmation is one of the borrowings from the Catholic Church.

   NOTE: The Protestants practice confirmation like the Catholics even as to the age at which it is done.

IV. Confirmation is mentioned in the Scriptures, but not as the institution practiced by either the Catholic or Protestant Churches.

THE BIBLE:

1. The apostles' preaching was "confirmed" by the signs which followed (Mark 16: 20).

   NOTE: These signs were: Speaking in tongues of other nations, healing the sick, performing miracles and raising the dead.

2. These signs were the credentials of the apostles (II Cor. 12: 12).
3. For any to receive confirmation today would be to give them power to perform the miracles the apostles did.
4. For any to claim such confirming signs today makes such false apostles because they are usurping the signs of an apostle (Matt. 7: 21-23; II Cor. 11: 13-15).
5. Paul speaks of the confirmation of the Gospel, which refers to the proving of the Gospel, not to a rite performed on some person (Phil. 1: 7).

V. The Catholic Church teaches that the Holy Spirit is given in confirmation.

"The bishop then offers a prayer, preceded by certain versicles—"Show us, O Lord, thy mercy and give us thy salvation . . . . O God, who hast given thy Holy Spirit to thy apostles, and hast willed that He should be given to the other faithful by them and their successors, regard benignantly the service of our lowliness; and grant that the same Holy Spirit, coming upon these whose foreheads we have anointed with holy chrism and marked with the sign of the cross." Ex. of C. C., Pp. 57, 58.

The Bible:

1. Christ is the only one who can pray the Holy Spirit to be sent (John 14: 15-17).
2. The Father is the only one who can confer the Holy Spirit (John 14: 15-17).
3. The Holy Spirit, as an indwelling Comforter, is promised when one obeys in baptism and not after some rite of confirmation (Acts 2: 38).
4. Only the apostles had the power to confer the Holy Spirit upon a person by the laying on of hands.
    (1.) There are only four cases of this and in each case it was done by the laying on of apostles' hands.

181

    a. The seven deacons by the apostles (Acts 6: 6).

    b. The Samaritans by Peter and John (Acts 8: 14-18).

    c. The Twelve Ephesians by Paul (Acts 19: 6, 7).

    d. Timothy by Paul's hands (II Tim. 1: 6).

(2.) A preacher, who was not an apostle, could not impart the Holy Spirit by the laying on of hands (Acts 8: 12-17).

(3.) Those who had apostle's hands laid on them could not impart the Holy Spirit to others (Acts 6: 6; 8: 12-17).

(4.) Only the apostles could impart the Holy Spirit by the laying on of hands (Acts 6: 6; 8: 14-17; 19: 6; II Tim. 1: 6).

5. Since only apostles could confer the gift of the Holy Spirit by the laying on of hands, and since the apostles could have no successors, then the Holy Spirit could not be conferred in confirmation by the laying on of hands.

(1.) Only one case of apostolic succession— Matthias succeeded Judas (Acts 1: 15-26).

(2.) The successor of an apostle must have companied with Christ from the baptism of John to the ascension of Christ (Acts 1: 21, 22).

(3.) When James was beheaded they did not meet and select one to take his place as in the case of Judas (Acts 2: 15-26; Acts 15: 1-29).

(4.) NOTE: None today could meet the requirements of an apostle or the successor to an apostle. An apostle is a witness of Christ's ministry and resurrection and a witness can have no successor.

Bibliography

ABBREVIATION

The Externals of the Catholic Church; Ex. C. C.
    Her Government, Ceremonies, Festi-
    vals, Sacramentals and Devotions.
        By John F. Sullivan.
Luther's Shorter Catechism L. S. C.
Historical Lutherism H. L.
Westminster Confession of Faith
Institutes—John Calvin.
General Assembly, Los Angeles, Cal.,
    1903.
Book of Common Prayer.
Christian Institutions,
        By Arthur P. Stanley.
Methodist Discipline or the Doctrines
    and Discipline of the Methodist Epis-
    copal Church.
Synopsis of Present Truth,
        Elder U. Smith.
Key of Theology.
Doctrine and Covenants, D. and C.
        Given to Joseph Smith, Jr., the
        Prophet.
Book of Mormon.
The Seer.
Journal of Discourses,
        Brigham Young.
Scripture Studies.
The Watch Tower.
Science and Health, 1917 Edition. S. and H.

CPSIA information can be obtained at www.ICGtesting.com
Printed in the USA
LVOW060433161211

259703LV00001B/3/A